The Spirit of Whiskey

History, Anecdotes, Trends and Cocktails

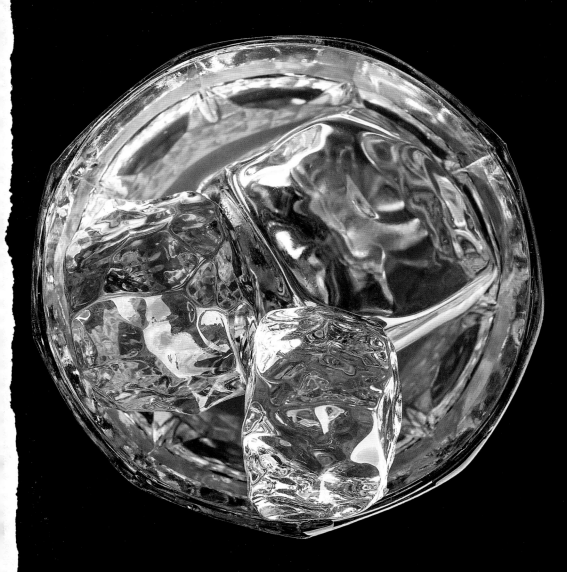

WHITE STAR PUBLISHERS

Contents

TEXT BY Claudio Riva and Davide Terziotti

PHOTOGRAPHS BY Fabio Petroni

COCKTAILS BY Erik Viola

Introduction

It can be said, without fear of contradiction, that whiskey is one of the most evocative alcoholic beverages, copiously exploited in cinematography, television series and literature. Stars like Humphrey Bogart and Frank Sinatra are immediately associated with whiskey, to the point that the famous singer was honored with a bottle produced by an equally evocative brand of Tennessee whiskey.

In many cultures whiskey is considered a rare pleasure, something to be savored slowly while the mind is transported to smoke-filled bars and gambling halls; to the Prohibition era in America; to aristocratic living rooms furnished with Chesterfield sofas or after dinner with friends when opening a bottle that has been sealed for who knows how long. In other societies it is considered a popular drink like wine or beer, available in abundance and at low prices, also to drink mixed and without reverential fear.

Like the life of the stars with whom it is often associated, the whiskey market and consumption experience both rapid rises and disastrous falls. If we looked at a graph starting from the end of the 19th century, we would see a high frequency of cycles where the industry expands rapidly and then falls just as quickly, contributed to by the disastrous effects of the two World Wars.

This up-and-down trend seems to have come to an end and the current period appears to be the most prosperous yet, with apparently unstoppable worldwide success. Magazines, festivals and books on whiskey proliferate and the amount of consumers, fans, collectors, writers and blog is increasing dramatically. Whiskey is a global phenomenon and as such cannot be reduced to pure evocation or informative articles in glossy magazines. The bottles presented in this book were selected to recount and above all highlight the many varieties and main differences that a consumer can find. Geographic diversity, much more evident in the past – with some exceptions – is now much reduced, and there are very different aromas and flavors within the same product category, or even in products from the same distillery. Even in countries that are considered more traditionalist, like Scotland, innovations have never stopped, in pursuit of both productive efficiency, in a period of high demand, and new consumers. Mixing, which often makes purists curl up their noses, is another important brick in this product's success. Types of whiskeys like rye, almost completely forgotten, are back in vogue thanks to the rediscovery of many classic cocktails. In the following pages, readers will have to free themselves from all their prejudices or inflexibility, bringing all their knowledge about whiskey into question.

History and Geography

The history of whiskey is often oversimplified with the use of graphical representations, exact dates and unreliable sources such as myths and legends. Tradition, for example, reputes that the first whiskey was distilled by St. Patrick when he returned to Ireland in 432 A.D., after having learnt the technique from Arab populations during his mission to spread Christianity.

At the dawn of distillation, spirits were generally referred to as *aqua vitae* (water of life), the same meaning as the term whiskey which derives from the Gaelic *uisge beatha*, and alcohol was

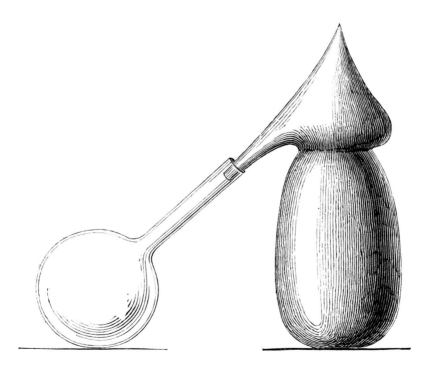

19th century reproduction of a drawing of a small alembic still invented by Zozimus of Panopolis in the 3rd century.

still primarily used for medicinal purposes. Alchemists were the most skilled in the art of distillation: Zosimus of Panopolis, a Greek alchemist who lived between the 3rd and 4th centuries, described distillation devices and drew them in detail in a drawing that has survived until today. One of the more noteworthy Arabic alchemists who played a key role in the perfection and diffusion of distillation in the 8th century, was Abu Moussah Dschabir al Soli, known as Geber, who described the equipment used for the distillation of rosewater, which together with rose oil was prescribed for the treatment of many ailments. After Geber, the technique was next documented by Abū Bakr Muhammad ibn Zakariyyā al-Rāzī, known by the Latin name of Rhazes, who lived at the turn of the 9th century, and the Syrian Ibn Sinā, better known as Avicenna (980-1037). Unequivocal evidence of how Arabs played a decisive role can also be found in linguistics: the origins of the words alcohol (*al-kuhl*) and alembic (*al-anbīq*) derive from Arabic, although it was Theophrastus Bombastus von Hohenheim, known as Paracelsus (1493-1541), who first used "alcohol" in the modern sense of the word. Arabic science passed this knowledge on through several institutions. One of these was the Schola Medica Salernitana, which from the 10th century onwards played a fundamental role and become a nexus of Arab and Byzantine-Greek culture.

In this context, whiskey remained primarily an agricultural product for a long time, obtained by using crop surpluses which often wouldn't keep for the following months, being used to barter for goods. Development in remote areas, away from governmental control, gave rise to the myth of bootleggers, moonshiners and smugglers.

Whiskey, in similar forms to today's spirit, only developed in the second half of the 1800s, when consumption began to increase alongside technological interventions to improve its quality and make production more efficient. In particular, the introduction of the column still and continuous distillation made it possible for whiskey to make a definitive leap into the industrial era.

Scotland

A symbolic date for Scotch whisky is June 1st, 1495, the date on an Exchequer Roll found at Lindores Abbey which notes that John Corr, a monk at the Abbey, was given eight bolls (old unit of measurement for grains) of malt to make *aqua vitae*. In 1505, the Guild of Surgeon Barbers in Edinburgh was granted a monopoly over the manufacture and commercialization of whisky – a fact that reflects that alcohol was valued for its medicinal properties. In 1540, parliament clearly separated the two professions, probably because they were aware of their dissimilarity. After decades of battles between government agencies, moonshiners and bootleggers, the Excise Tax Act in 1823, promoted by the Duke of Gordon, was perhaps what established peace and restored the legality of most distillers. The industrial revolution had reached its peak and communication routes had improved, mainly thanks to new railways and shipping routes. The optimism that generated around Industrial Production also whet the minds of inventors. In 1826, Robert Stein perfected the first distillation column, which was much more efficient than the traditional alembic pot still and able to produce a far more drinkable distilled spirit. In 1830, this alembic was further improved by Aeneas Coffey, an Irish excise officer, who gave his name to the invention: the Coffey Still. While the Irish refused to adopt this new technology, the Scottish embraced it enthusiastically. This is when the first great merchants appeared, buying whiskies from the distillers and selling them in their stores. During this period, legendary whiskies produced by brands such as Ballantine's, Chivas, Dewar's and Johnny Walker became widespread, and consequently so did the first "blenders" to have the intuition to create a recipe and make recognizable and repeatable products by mixing different whiskies. Product specifications and government regulations encouraged this practice. The Phylloxera, an aphid from the New World, also came to the aid of whisky producers. At the time, cognac was still the finest and most consumed distilled spirit on the tables of Britain's high society. Most of the vineyards were destroyed in the 1860s, immediately affecting wine and a few years

later cognac, resulting in the precious French distilled spirit being replaced with Scotch. In 1877, the Distillers Company was founded, initially formed by a combination of six Scotch whisky distilleries and then acquiring several other producers over the following years. The United States also began to import whisky, even if the long Prohibition era abruptly halted the diffusion of alcoholic beverages. Throughout this period, Scotch whisky had a very bad reputation, fueled by scandals and adulterated products that even led to a long series of deaths.

In the years that coincided with the beginning of the First World War, the abuse of low quality alcohol, together with fears concerning the effects on public order, led the authorities to introduce a minimum maturation period of two years in wooden barrels – later increased to three – convinced that it would reduce aggressive behavior if whisky was finished and polished while maturing in wood.

Advertisement for Johnnie Walker in a British magazine
in around 1890.

The single malt distilleries that opened, closed and reopened in the following years, were all at the service of blenders. Each distillery produced a distilled spirit with unusual characteristics that were functional to the recipe of famous blend brands. It was only in the 1950s that single malt whisky moved away from being a niche ingredient. The roles of buyer and independent bottler were perfected. Great Scottish merchants like Cadenhead's, Gordon & MacPhail's and Douglas Laing began to sell single malt whisky more frequently or, along with many other distilleries, to sell their product to famous buyers such as Silvano Samaroli or importers like Rinaldi. One of the most important figures in the success of single malt whisky was Charles Gordon, descendant of the Grant family – owners of Glenfiddich – who in the 1960s gave a decisive impetus to the valorization and protection of single malt whiskies.

After the optimism of the 1960s and 70s, which led to the construction of numerous new distilleries, 1983 proved to be whisky's *annus horribilis*: overproduction and a consequent drop in consumption led to a crisis dubbed the "Whisky Loch." But the setback, however disastrous, didn't last long. The rise was fast and Scotch whisky quickly became a global phenomenon. The very strict product specification for Scotch whisky, protected by the Scotch Whisky Association, recognizes two major categories of Scotch whisky: malt whisky and grain whisky. The first must be produced from malted barley by batch distillation in pot stills, while the remaining types fall under the grain whisky category. Combinations of these two types form the five categories of Scotch whisky: single malt, malt whisky produced at a single distillery, and single grain, grain whisky also produced at a single distillery; blended malt, which is a mixture of single malt whiskies; blended grain, a blend of single grain whiskies; and finally, blended, a mixture of malt and grain whiskies. All products can be colored with E150 caramel coloring.

Tasting in an aging warehouse
at the Glenfiddich Distillery.

Ireland

For a long time, Irish whiskey had a far higher reputation than its Scottish counterparts, which were more likely to produce low quality and often adulterated distilled spirits.

The first written evidence of whiskey in Ireland dates back to 1405: in the annals of the small village of Clonmacnoise, the death of a clan chief is attributed to an "excess of *aqua vitae*." Queen Elizabeth I and the Russian Tsar Peter the Great were both very fond of Irish whiskey. The first blow to contribute to its decline ironically came from an Irishman, excise officer Aeneas Coffey, who filed a patent for the so-called "patent still", a two-column alembic that made continuous distillation possible, the exact opposite of the traditional discontinuous alembic. Coffey perfected the invention of two of his predecessors, Anthony Perrier and Robert Stein. The growth of Scotch whisky produced with a continuous alembic began to affect the export of Irish whiskey across the world.

The Irish refused to accept the situation and tried to question the legitimacy of producing whiskey with an alembic that was different to the traditional one, and in 1879 they published a book called "Truths about Whiskey." In 1909, the Royal Commission on Whiskey and other Potable Spirits definitively rejected their petition. Irish whiskey almost disappeared with the arrival of Prohibition, World War I and the Irish War of Independence. In 1966, the three surviving distilleries in the Republic of Ireland, John Jameson & Son, John Power & Son and the Cork Distillery Company (owner of the Old Midleton distillery), joined forces and formed the Irish Distillers Group, transferring production to a single, large distillery – New Midleton – where the use of column stills and the production of blended whiskey ignited the rebirth of the Irish whiskey industry. This rebirth continued with Cooley in 1987, followed by plans to build many other distilleries.

Advertising poster for whiskey produced by the Old Bushmills distillery, founded in 1608.

Whiskey or Whisky?

The word whisk(e)y is the English form of the ancient Gaelic expression *uisce beatha* or *uisge-beatha,* literally "water of life." We often see the word written in two different ways: whiskey and whisky. Although we generally say that Ireland and the United States use the whiskey form, while the rest of the world opts for whisky, it isn't actually so clear-cut.

Why the difference? It now seems well established that the Irish systematically introduced this differentiation during the 19th century to distinguish themselves from Scotch producers. However, in the meantime there were Irish producers who still continued to use the traditional form, and Scots that used the "Irish" form.

The influx of Irish distillers in the United States was undoubtedly responsible for the extra "e" arriving on the other side of the Atlantic, although it is uncertain whether it was actually the Irish in America who introduced the said "e." Can we therefore conclude that all U.S. producers and official documents use whiskey? No, that would be too simple. The main brands have adopted it, but even in the product specification that regulates the production of American whiskey, the legal term is "whisky", although the whiskey form may be freely used. In Japan both terms are found on the labels.

It all just seems to create more confusion. In short, the two forms could be considered interchangeable; whiskey is more generic, and for this reason we have chosen to use it in this book.

United States

The first American whiskey was probably a rye whiskey, and the first distillers were most likely Central European immigrants who arrived in Pennsylvania during the 18th and 19th centuries, often Germans and Moravians fleeing from religious persecution. The area between the Appalachian and Allegheny mountains was the cradle of American whiskey, which was transported via the Ohio River. The use of rye was not a random choice: it was a common grain in the distillers' homelands and also widely used for breadmaking. Herbs or fruit were often added to the distilled spirit. The enormous national debt following the 1776 War of Independence was in the hands of several European banks.

They tried to introduce a direct tax on the production of spir-

Anti-government cartoon depicting the 1794 Whiskey Rebellion in Pennsylvania.

Drawing of the funeral of a bottle of whiskey at the beginning of Prohibition in America, drawn by Achille Beltrame in 1919.

its but the distillers rebelled and refused to pay, partly because a large part of their economy was barter-based rather than monetary. This was the beginning of the "Whiskey Rebellion." After negotiations failed, President George Washington called forth the army to subdue the rebellion, with himself riding at the head of the troops, and succeeded in suppressing it. The tax was never fully redeemed and was eventually revoked in 1801. Rye whiskey continued to be the true American spirit until the 20th century, when it was almost completely supplanted by Bourbon.

Prohibition, implemented with the Volstead Act and the Eighteenth Amendment between 1919 and 1933, declared a ban on the manufacture, sale, import and transportation of alcohol, and had a devastating effect on whiskey producers, contributing to the decline of rye whiskeys. The first day without legal alcohol was 20th January 1920, and the long "dry" period reduced consumption by 50% right up until 1940. An unusual world-leading phenomenon, which has developed over the last few decades, is that of craft micro-distilleries, which are catching the wave of craft breweries. This phenomenon started on the West Coast in 1993, when Steve McCarthy founded the Clear Creek Distillery in Portland, and – almost simultaneously – Fritz Maytag opened Anchor Distilling in San Francisco. These two names have now been joined by several hundred distilleries that have started to develop and experiment with innovative production systems, mainly concentrated in Kentucky, seeking to turn the tables on major producers.

In recent years, alongside the whirlwind growth of micro-distilleries and Bourbon, rye whiskey has also made a comeback after having almost disappeared from store shelves and bars. An aggressive comeback, with triple-digit growth, probably triggered by the spark created by the world of mixology, together with the rediscovery of "old fashioned" cocktails like – naturally – the Old Fashioned or the Manhattan, which have been in vogue since rye whiskey has been the king of whiskeys.

American legislation is pretty complex. A whiskey can only be called Bourbon if the mash bill (mix of grains) contains at least 51% corn and is left to ferment in charred and new oak barrels. The word "straight" indicates that the product has been aged at least two years, and all bourbons aged less than four years must bear an age statement. Other rules for it to be considered a Bourbon are that it cannot be distilled over 80% alcohol-by-volume, it must be put into a barrel for ageing at no more than 62.5% ABV, and it must be bottled at no less than 40% ABV. The same applies to rye whiskey (mash bill containing at least 51% rye) and wheat whiskeys (mash bill containing at least 51% wheat).

Japan

The Japanese have been distilling spirits from grains for centuries, but Japan's self-imposed isolation in 1633 prohibited all contact with the outside world. On June 8th, 1853, U.S. Commodore Matthew Calbraith Perry illegally entered Tokyo Bay and initiated negotiations, offering several gifts to facilitate the process, including, it seems, some whisky. Although the Japanese ordered Perry not to return, he came back six months later with a larger fleet, carrying several gallons of whisky for the Emperor and other officials to promote negotiations. On March 31st, 1854, the United States and Japan signed the Kanagawa Treaty, officially establishing peace and amity between the two nations. A period of reform began after the Shogunate was abolished in 1868, and news of a "Western liquor" (*yoshu*) began to spread, arousing curiosity. The first attempts to reproduce this drink that almost nobody knew about were made during this time of renewal and reform. Alcohol was still considered medicinal, therefore until 1901 it was very simple to get around the tax. From 1901, the production of alcohol started to be regulated and they started importing the first continuous stills from Europe. The two main producers, Nikka and Suntory, told different stories about what happened next, both of which unilaterally magnified their founders. It is therefore necessary to take a step backwards and look at it from a different angle.

Undoubtedly, the first key figure in the birth of Japanese whisky was Shinjiro Torii, who perfected his knowledge on Western alcoholic drinks by first working in a liquor store and then, in 1899, running one himself, which he later named Kotobukiya. His desire to experiment and find a flavor that would please Japanese taste buds, led him to try mixing different alcoholic drinks together and become increasingly interested in the West. In 1907, he found a recipe that he was satisfied with and he called the product – a sweet wine – Akadama Port wine.

The wine met with success and prompted Shinjiro to create something similar to a whisky.

By this time, Torii was convinced that he could create a whisky that would satisfy Japanese tastes and he began to think about opening a distillery.

The second key figure is Masataka Taketsuru, the son of the owner of a sake brewery and a chemistry student. In 1917, he joined the Settsu Shuzo liquor company and Torii and Taketsuru probably met at this juncture. Kihei Abe, the owner of Settsu Shuzo, decided to send someone to Scotland to study the art of whisky-making and he chose Taketsuru, who embarked in 1918. During his time in Scotland he met his wife Rita, who became a key figure in both his life and career. In the 1920s, after his Scottish apprenticeship and marriage to Rita, Taketsuru returned to Japan. Meanwhile Torii's company Kotobukiya was preparing to open the first Japanese whisky distillery in the village of Yamazaki, near Kyoto, and the official date of the first distillation was November 11th, 1924. Taketsuru was hired shortly beforehand and became part of the venture as the distillery manager. The first whisky was launched in April 1929, with the name Suntory Shirofuda (white label), but after a few months Taketsuru and Torii went their separate ways. After going through a difficult period, Taketsuru began a new adventure and founded the Yoichi distillery in Hokkaido, a place that reminded him of Scotland. It became the second largest group in Japan: Nikka. The rest is an overwhelming story of successes which were rewarded in 2001, when Yoichi 10 won the "Best of the Best" award in a blind tasting organized by Whisky Magazine.

In Japan there is no regulation on whisky, so any kind of drink can be labelled as such. There is no geographical protection like there is for Scotch whisky, therefore any type of imported whisky can be labelled as Japanese; there are no strict regu-

Seiichi Koshimizu, famous Chief Blender at Suntory Yamazaki.

lations on aging, any type of container can be used, and furthermore, there is no specified minimum age, so even a distilled spirit that has just come out of the alembic can be called whisky; there is no limitation on the minimum alcohol strength, which can therefore be below 40%, the minimum standard for many regulated markets; the recipe does not necessarily have to derive from the fermentation of grains alone, it can be mixed with other types of alcohol with different origins and can also be aromatized. Although there is no regulation, for Single Malts the distilleries adopt the same rules used in Scotland, and therefore there is a greater guarantee of authenticity.

Rest of the World

Whiskey production is now widespread throughout the world and there are many whiskey producing countries. Not everywhere has an exact definition for the use of the term whiskey, which means that a product that is a whiskey in one country, may not be called that in other geographical areas. European legislation used Scotland as an example and requires that whiskey be matured for at least three years in wooden casks of a capacity not exceeding 700 liters (185 US gal), whereby imported whiskeys must also adhere to labelling requirements. France, which is also one of the main consumer countries, is growing exponentially and the country is now dotted with new distilleries, or distilleries of other spirits that are also producing whiskey.

Buyers and Independent Bottlers

The owners of distilleries, which in recent decades have passed increasingly into the hands of multinational companies, have only recently started to promote and market single malt whiskeys directly. For most of whiskey's recent history, which began in the mid-1800s, the commerce and success of it depended on the blenders, who created their whiskey by buying the "ingredients" from distilleries and proposing their own recipe. The big brands that emerged under the control of the so-called "Whiskey Barons" – Walker, Dewar, Buchanan and Haig – are from this period. Asides from the blenders, another important role was played by "independent" figures: brokers, who still commercialize large quantities of whiskey today, and merchants, who bought barrels so they could fill them with their own brand. Their warehouses gradually filled up with large quantities of barrels and their business began to grow: Cadenhead, founded in 1842, and Gordon & MacPhail, established as a grocery business in 1895, are just two of these companies which are still in business today. Buyers appeared on the scene after the Second World War, due to the wide availability of unusual, rare products that were aged for long periods of time. Whereas brokers and traders mainly dealt in buying stock, buyers took advantage of the large number of barrels to choose the very best and then sign them. This consequently led to small batches and "signed" bottles. Thanks to names like Samaroli, Intertrade, Giaccone, Sestante, Rinaldi and Giovinetti, Italy has been at the vanguard of buyers and importers. As a result of this, the world of collections was developed in Italy by names like Zagatti, Giaccone, Casari, Begnoni and D'Ambrosio. The importance of these independent figures in the development of Scotch whisky has been decisive, and many single malts whiskeys, some belonging to distilleries that have been closed for decades, are well-known and have survived until today mainly thanks to the great work of these people and companies. There is only one reason why buyers' whiskeys have not been included in this book: they are, with some exceptions, limited editions sold in small batches, and they often disappear very quickly from the shelves.

Whiskey and False Myths

Whiskey's history is steeped in clichés, legends or even just legacies from the past, now outdated in a fast-moving world. Whiskey itself, perceived as a traditional product, has also changed enormously over the last few decades, and general rules that were once valid now have much less clear-cut boundaries.

The older it is, the better it is

Long maturation periods do not guarantee quality, although they do affect the price due to their rarity. During maturation, the whiskey extracts substances from the wood and a measure of its volume of alcohol is lost, known as "The Angels' Share." If these two processes are excessive, the whiskey could lose quality, especially on the palate: the wood can become overpowering by yielding bitter notes and also adding astringency due to tannins. Peat whiskeys lose their freshness and their characteristic peaty note weakens: peated whiskeys are at their peak when they reach 8 to 12 years of age.

Whiskey is expensive

You can buy an excellent whiskey for a few tens of dollars, and it is no coincidence that many of the labels in this book were chosen because they are easily accessible. If stored correctly, a bottle can be kept at home for several months, and a dram costs just a few dollars. If you go out, and not necessarily to a specialized bar, with very little money you can get immense satisfaction.

The darker it is, the better it tastes

The color of a distilled spirit, or wine and beer for that matter, greatly influences consumer choice. A dark color impresses the consumer, triggering synesthesia that leads him or her to associate it with long periods of aging and barrels laden with aromas that determine the distilled spirit. As whiskey is often used as a digestive after dinner, a dark distilled spirit is considered more full-bodied and persistent; a perfect meditation drink. Color is certainly an indicator of the type of cask used for aging, but it is often misleading. A whisky aged in Taiwan, in a tropical climate, will acquire a much deeper color than a whiskey aged in the same type of cask in the cold and humid Scottish climate. A barrel used previously for Pedro Ximenez Sherry imparts an almost mahogany shade, while Bourbon-matured whiskey can acquire dark golden yellow hues. The "artificial" colors that are obtained with caramel coloring, permitted for some types of whiskey, must also be taken into consideration.

All Scotch whisky is peated

If it was the 1960s, there would probably be grounds for this assumption. Peat was widely used in the malting process and many whiskies often had a peaty note as a side effect. With the advent of the industrialization of malting and the improvement of production techniques, peat is now only where you want it to be and – when it's there – it is also perceived much more clearly. There are only a few distilleries that continue to produce peated whisky and they represent a small slice of the market, below 10% of the total. Peat is therefore an exception.

There are no peated Irish whiskeys

This belief stems from the evolution of the history of Irish whiskey, but after its rebirth there are many expressions of Irish whiskey that can easily be exchanged for some of the most famous peated Scotch whiskies. One example is the Cooley distillery, which produces the Connemara brand.

Never serve with water or ice

With its strict rules and regulations, whiskey is often perceived as a distilled spirit for "connoisseurs." Of course there are rules on how to serve a perfect dram: the choice of glass, serving temperature and accompanying water. The tumbler is a bad glass for fully appreciating whiskey. Ice blunts the flavors and aromas. However, if on a hot summer's day you want to add a little ice to a good Bourbon, maybe with a splash of soda and served in an Old Fashioned glass, why not? Or how about serving Japanese whisky with soda in a highball? The cocktail recipes in this book will certainly help you uncover a totally different world from the one you have always imagined.

Around the World in 40 Whiskeys

There are many types of whiskey, differing according to the ingredients and production process, and even when they are defined by a strict product specification, the end results can be very different.
The choice of labels in this book was aimed at covering the widest range of types of whiskey, in addition to highlighting the differences.
The bottles have been grouped into three categories which focus on the particularities of the ingredients, distillation and maturation. In each category, the bottles are grouped by producer country.

Ingredients

BenRiach Curiositas 10

Kilkerran 12

Kilchoman 100% Islay (8th edition)

Highland Park 10 Old Viking Scars

Ben Nevis 10

Bruichladdich Bere Barley 2009

Green Spot Single Pot Still

Connemara 12

Widow Jane Straight Bourbon

Koval Four Grain

Sonoma 2nd Chance Wheat

Four Roses Single Barrel

Masterson's 10 Years Old Straight Rye

Chichibu The Floor Malted

Eddu Silver

Slyrs Single Malt

Three main ingredients are used to produce whiskey: water, grains and yeast. Whiskey travels along the same tracks as beer for most of its journey, sharing part of the ingredients and production process, until it veers off and takes its own path.

Water

This is the main ingredient and is used throughout the process. With the modernization and improvement of yeasts and grains, its composition and characteristics, unique to each area, have gradually lost importance. Of course there are some whiskeys whose characteristics derive from water or valorize its origin: Widow Jane, for example, uses water from the Widow Jane Mine, and Talisker acquires its savory notes from the springs on the Isle of Skye, but generally a distillery needs to use a spring that is abundant and available year-round. A distillery cannot operate without water and all modern distilleries have improved the process by trying not to waste it. As the old Scottish proverb goes, "Today's rain is tomorrow's whiskey."

Yeast

In the production process, yeast, which is part of the Fungi kingdom, is perhaps one of the least known ingredients considered by non-experts. In some respects it is a paradox, because potable alcohol cannot be produced without yeast. It is even more paradoxical if we think that in beer production yeast often has a central role in determining the aromatic profile of the final product. With the improvement of knowledge and the search for better productivity, or yield, which measures the amount of alcohol anhydrous per ton of grain, yeasts have gradually been specialized.

Many distilleries use yeast strains that are specifically selected for distillation. There are still distilleries which have remained faithful to the use of brewer's yeast, like Ben Nevis, or which grow their own yeasts. In fact, yeasts "eat" sugar and turn it into alcohol and carbon dioxide.

Grains

Grains provide "fuel" and food for yeast. Pseudograins, plants that are not part of the grass family yet have all the same characteristics, are also permitted: Eddu Breton whiskey, for example, uses buckwheat. Barley is considered the main grain, one of the reasons being that it can be malted more easily than, for example, corn. It is precisely for this reason that we refer to malted barley when we talk about malt whiskey.

Whiskey is actually a beer that is subsequently distilled. The first stage therefore consists of producing a sweet wort from the naturally occurring starch found in grain. As yeasts are unable to metabolize complex sugars, starch has to be converted in to sugar before it can be used for fermentation.

To start the fermentation process, the mixture of grain must therefore contain "malt", which activates the naturally occurring enzymes within the grain. The malt is obtained through a completely natural process that takes place inside the grain kernel, activating the germination. The grain is wet and the plant, as it starts to develop, promotes the conversion of starch into maltose. There are enzymes that can be added to facilitate this process, although this practice is prohibited in Scotch whisky and therefore only naturally-occurring enzymes in malted grains can be utilized.

Malt can be produced in the traditional way, as is still the case in some distilleries, such as Balvenie, Highland Park, Springbank, Bowmore and Laphroaig, or in industrial plants.

Traditional malting takes place on a malting floor. The barley grains are soaked in water, spread out on the floor and then turned continuously for a few days; this stage requires a lot of manpower. The humidity promotes the germination of the kernels and the conversion of starch into maltose. After a few days the malted barley is moved onto perforated floors through which hot air passes, blocking germination and maximizing the presence of simple sugars. During the drying stage it is possible to infuse the still-wet malt with peat smoke (or other fuels such as wood) to give it the characteristic smoky aroma that is eventually found in the bottle. The smokiness is expressed as phenol parts per million (ppm) of the malted barley. The steps are the same in the industrial process, but the stage in which the barley is turned on the malting floor, which requires more manpower, is carried out by huge rotating metal cylinders. Whereas malt whiskeys are made with a recipe that only uses malted barley, there is also a wide variety of whiskeys that use other grains. Bourbons are typically made up of corn, rye whiskeys of rye and wheat whiskeys of wheat, but there are also many whiskeys that us oats or millet.

Another aspect to bear in mind is the search for greater productivity, which has made grains an anonymous ingredient without any indication of origin, often to the detriment of local varieties or ancestral grains with a low yield. In recent years, this homogenization has been challenged, with some producers returning to abandoned grain varieties or promoting the origin of the grains. Bruichladdich was on the front line in this battle for the terroir. Many American distilleries, for example Koval and Widow Jane, use niche or organic grains, while the Slyrs distillery boasts about its use of Bavarian barley for its single malt whiskeys.

BenRiach
Curiositas 10

Features: *Speyside peat.*

Country: *Scotland (Speyside)*
Producer: *BenRiach Distillery*
ABV: *46%* • **Bottle:** *70 cl*

Typology: *Single Malt Scotch whisky*
Production: *double distillation in copper alembic stills.*

The BenRiach Distillery is in Longmorn, in the heart of the Speyside area, and was founded in 1897 by John Duff. It closed after just 3 years and was not reopened again until 1965. For many years it remained in the shadows, producing almost exclusively blended whisky. In 2004, it was bought by the South African group Intra Trading, and thanks to the decisive contribution of Billy Walter, who had many years of experience behind him working at the Chivas Bros and Burn Stewart distilleries, it began to commercialize Single Malts, creating a wide and varied range of products. A few years ago, the distillery started its own floor maltings again, after stopping in 1998, albeit very sporadically.

BenRiach only dedicates a small part of its production to whisky made with malted barley peated at 35ppm, a practice it started in 1983. Curiositas 10 has a profile that is quite different from its Islay counterparts, as the Speyside peat gives the whisky more vegetal notes and less maritime elements. It therefore sets an excellent benchmark for many other peated whiskies on the market, maintaining the constant freshness of a young peated whisky without the sea saltiness of whiskies like Lagavulin.

Tasting
Nose: *grass and smoke, with notes of marzipan and honey*
Palate: *grains, candied sugar, nuts, peppercorn, grass and notes of charred wood*
Finish: *woody, fresh and grassy*

Kilkerran 12

Features: *floor malted barley.*

Country: *Scotland (Campbeltown)*
Producer: *Glengyle Distillery*
ABV: *46%* • **Bottle:** *70 cl*

Typology: *Single Malt Scotch whisky*
Production: *double distillation in copper alembic stills.*

The whisky producing regions of Scotland are now somewhat obsolete but they are still an excellent marketing vehicle and tool for immediate divulgation. In the early 2000s, there were only two active distilleries in Campbeltown: Springbank and Glen Scotia. The Scotch Whisky Association, which defines the product specification, proposed that Campbeltown be removed from the list of Scotch whisky producing regions, as it was included when the area still had dozens of distilleries. The Mitchell family, the owners of Springbank, decided to revive the name and building of an old distillery in the area that had been closed since 1925, investing over four million pounds and thereby bringing the number of distilleries in Campbeltown up to three – on a par with the Lowlands – saving the area from the dishonor of being removed from the list. The building project was entrusted entirely to former master distiller Frank McHardy. The Glengyle distillery started production in 2004, and the Single Malt whiskies were released with the name Kilkerran, the original name of Campbeltown, as the Glengyle brand belongs to another distiller. The distillery is operated by the Springbank distillery workers.

The 12-year-old was the first whisky released, made from floor malted barley from the nearby Springbank distillery. It's lightly peated, non-chill filtered and was matured in a combination of 70% bourbon casks and 30% Sherry casks.

Tasting
Nose: *bacon, ash, peaty with maritime notes*
Palate: *salt, sultana, honey, ginger*
Finish: *long, earthy with spicy and smoky notes*

Kilchoman 100% Islay (8th edition)

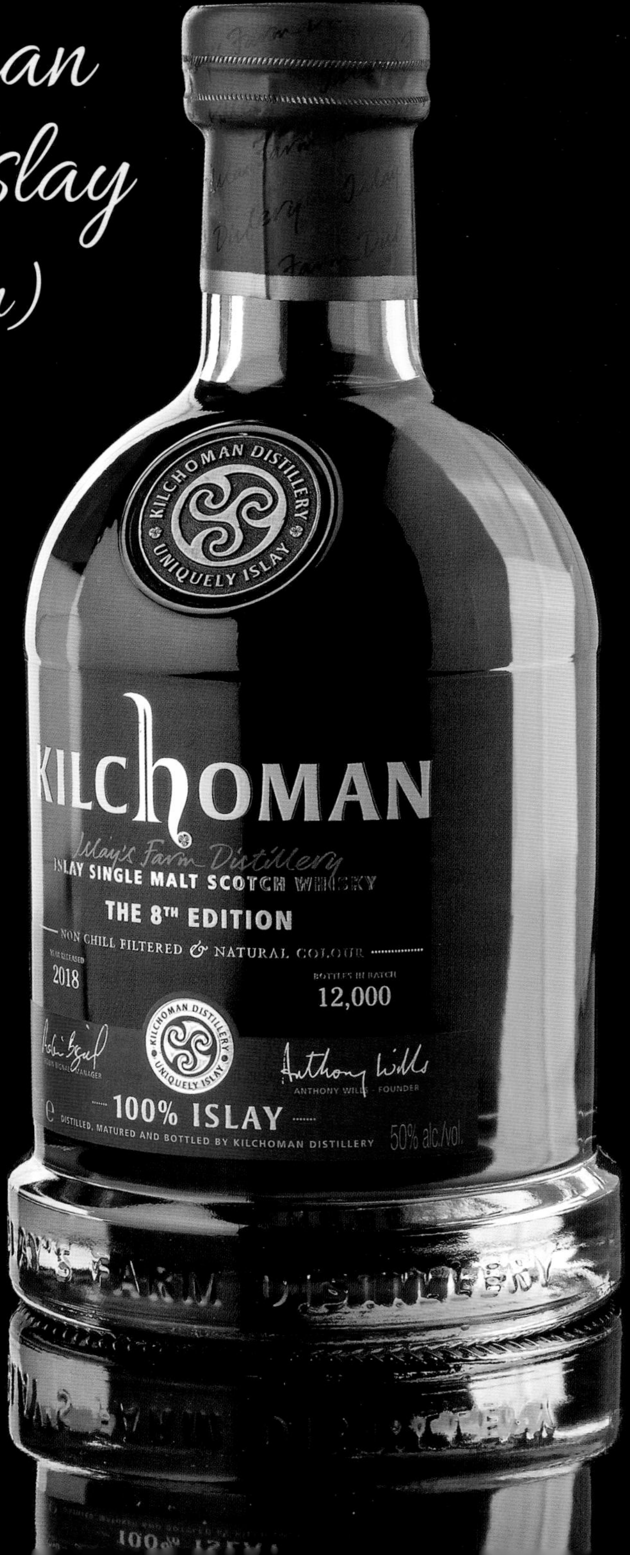

KILCHOMAN

Islay's Farm Distillery

ISLAY SINGLE MALT SCOTCH WHISKY

THE 8TH EDITION

NON CHILL FILTERED & NATURAL COLOUR

2018

BOTTLES IN BATCH
12,000

100% ISLAY

DISTILLED, MATURED AND BOTTLED BY KILCHOMAN DISTILLERY   50% alc./vol.

Features: *farm distillery, peat, floor malting, use of local grains, long fermentation times.*

Country: *Scotland (Islay)* **Typology:** *Single Malt Scotch whisky*
Producer: *Kilchoman Distillery* **Production:** *double distillation in copper*
ABV: *50%* • **Bottle:** *70 cl* *alembic stills.*

The Kilchoman distillery was inaugurated at the end of 2005, over 120 years after the last distillery opened on the island of Islay.

Kilchoman is a rather unique farm distillery in Scotland. It is situated on Rockside farm and is surrounded by fields of barley, which it uses for part of its production as it has a malting floor, expanded in 2018. The distillery doesn't directly face the sea, although its whiskies are greatly influenced by the Atlantic Ocean which lies just a few hundred meters away off the west coast. Since it opened, the distillery's goal has been to produce a Single Malt whisky that is associated as much as possible to Islay. Much of the barley comes from the fields bordering the distillery and this link strengthened in 2015, when Kilchoman announced that it had purchased all of Rockside farm.

The 100% Islay is the maximum expression of this agricultural spirit: 100% local, from the fields to the bottle, it is released annually in a limited edition. The first edition dates back to 2011. While Kilchoman's regular whiskies, made with malt from Port Ellen Maltings, have a peating level of 50ppm, the whisky made with floor malted barley reaches a level of about 20ppm. The eighth edition is a vatting of 23 bourbon barrels and 7 Oloroso sherry butts, filled between 2008 and 2012, and a total of 12,000 bottles have been released. It is neither artificially colored nor chill-filtered.

Tasting 8th Edition
Nose: *spices, wood, smoky*
Palate: *lemon, vanilla, cocoa, BBQ, nuts*
Finish: *honey, spices, smoky*

Highland Park 10 Old

Viking Scars

Features: *peat, floor malting.*

Country: *Scotland (Highlands)*
Producer: *Highland Park Distillery*
ABV: *40%* • **Bottle:** *70 cl*

Typology: *Single Malt Scotch whisky*
Production: *double distillation in copper alembic stills.*

Situated on the Orkney Islands, Highland Park, founded in 1798, is one of the few remaining distilleries that uses floor malting, even if it is only about 30% self-sufficient and buys a good part of its malted barley from large scale industrial maltings. All the peated barley used by the distillery is produced on site, using Orkney peat. Although it is an island peat, it is totally different from that of Islay, with earthier and sweeter notes. The peat is dug from beds that can be as deep as four meters and which are thousands of years old, and is much more compact and less oily than its counterpart.

Highland Park has five malting floors and dries the wet malt over a peat-heated fire for 18 hours before completing the drying process over a coal-heated fire. The malt peated to 35/40ppm is then mixed with unpeated malt bought from external suppliers and then peated to about 10ppm.

The 10-year-old whisky, which like so many other of the distillery's whiskies pays homage the "Viking" world that influenced these islands so much, perfectly expresses the spirit of the product, with rounded yet not too overpowering smoky notes. The maturation process takes place exclusively in Sherry casks, one of the distillery's distinctive characteristics.

Tasting

Nose: *citrus fruit, heather, earthy and maritime notes*
Palate: *citrus fruit, vanilla, maritime and spicy notes*
Finish: *sea salt, spices and a touch of iodine*

MACDONALD'S

BEN NEVIS

Ten Years Old
Highland Single Malt
Scotch Whisky

ESTABLISHED
1825

PRODUCT OF
SCOTLAND

AGED **10** YEARS

BEN NEVIS DISTILLERY (FORT WILLIAM) LIMITED
LOCHY BRIDGE, FORT WILLIAM PH33 6TJ, SCOTLAND

70cl   DISTILLED & BOTTLED IN SCOTLAND   46%vol

Ben Nevis 10

Features: *brewer's yeast, long fermentation time.*

Country: *Scotland (Highlands)*
Producer: *Ben Nevis Distillery*
ABV: *46%* • **Bottle:** *70 cl*

Typology: *Single Malt Scotch whisky*
Production: *double distillation in copper alembic stills.*

In 1825, 'Long' John McDonald requested a license for his distillery, Ben Nevis, on the outskirts of Fort William, which is near the highest mountain in the UK, namely Ben Nevis (1344 m – 4,413 ft). At the end of the 19th century, Ben Nevis's Long John's Dew blended whisky was a well-known brand, so much so, that a second distillery was built, the Nevis, although this then closed in 1908. In 1955, a Coffey still was introduced, making it the first Scottish distillery to be able to distill both grain and malt whisky. Unlike other distilleries, Hobbs began to age malt whisky and grain whisky together, mixing them before they were put in the barrels. The Coffey still was used for 26 long years. In 1989, the distillery was bought by the Japanese company Nikka, which had been buying Ben Nevis whisky to use in its blends for many years.

The 10-year-old was the first whisky released under the distillery's label in 1996, and the combination of Bourbon and Sherry casks give it great complexity. The quality and distinctive character of this whisky is also due to the particular attention Ben Nevis pays to the fermentation. Before micro-distilleries came on the scene, Ben Nevis was the last distillery in Scotland to use brewer's yeast instead of the more "modern" distiller's yeast, which is much more profitable. This particular yeast, together with extremely long fermentation times, gives Ben Nevis whiskies a wide range of aromas and flavors.

Tasting

Nose: *fruit, orange marmalade, nuts*
Palate: *sweet, notes of red fruit, toffee, custard, a light smoky note*
Finish: *dry with notes of coffee and chocolate*

Bruichladdich
Bere
Barley
2009

PROGRESSIVE HEBRIDEAN
DISTILLERS

BRUICHLADDIC

BERE
BARLEY
2009

WEYLAND & WATERSFIELD,
RICHMOND VILLA, QUOYBERSTANE &
NORTHFIELD FARMS. ORKNEY.

IT IS OUR MISSION TO
PURSUE THE ULTIMATE
PEDIGREE, PROVENANCE
AND TRACEABILITY OF
OUR RAW MATERIALS -
CHIEF OF WHICH IS OUR
BARLEY - AND TO PUSH
THE BOUNDARIES OF THE
CONCEPT OF TERROIR IN
ARTISANAL SINGLE
MALT WHISKY.

50% vol.
50% alc./vol.

UNPEATED
ISLAY SINGLE MALT
SCOTCH WHISKY

DISTILLED, MATURED AND BOTTLED,
UN-CHILL FILTERED AND COLOURING-FREE
AT BRUICHLADDICH DISTILLERY,
ISLE OF ISLAY, SCOTLAND.
PRODUCT OF SCOTLAND.

Features: *ancient barley, unpeated whiskey from the island of Islay.*

Country: *Scotland (Highlands)* **Typology:** *Single Malt Scotch whisky*
Producer: *Bruichladdich Distillery* **Production:** *double distillation in copper*
ABV: *46%* • **Bottle:** *70 cl* *alembic stills.*

Bruichladdich was founded in 1881, although like many other distilleries it suffered greatly, closing and reopening several times up until the year 2000. After years of suffering and neglect, Bruichladdich owes its rebirth to a group of investors headed by Jim McEwan, who after a lifetime at Bowmore decided to branch out on his own and reopen the distillery. Its marketing strategies and modern approach, as stated in the distillery's motto "Progressive · Hebridean · Distillers", put it under the spotlight. After twelve years, Bruichladdich was earning profit and was sold at a very high price to the Rémy Cointreau group. The distillery has always distinguished itself for its elegant, unpeated whisky, a characteristic that has been maintained, although now joined by new types of whisky produced from experimenting with different types of barrels, and the introduction of peated whisky packaged under the Octomore and Port Charlotte brands. Bruichladdich still represents the soul of Islay, providing work to many people: it was the first to believe in local barley and made a decisive contribution to increasing the amount of cultivated land. In fact, to promote the terroir, when it produces whisky with local barley or ancient barley such as Bere, it names the farm where the grain came from. What makes Bere different? Barley is often categorized into two groups: two-row and six-row, based on the number of rows of grains on the ear. Two-row barley has lower protein and higher sugar content, and therefore a higher spirit yield. Bere is an ancient six-row barley, presumed to have been introduced into the Orkneys in the 9th century by northern populations. It was gradually abandoned, leaving room for more profitable hybrids. The barley in the 2009 release comes from the Weyland & Watersfield, Richmond Villa, Quoyberstane and Northfield farms, all on the Orkney Islands.

Tasting
Nose: *floral, notes of vanilla, malt and wood*
Palate: *citrus fruit, pastry cream, vanilla, dry biscuits*
Finish: *grassy, creamy and citrusy*

Green Spot
Single Pot Still

Features: *uses unmalted barley.*

Country: *Ireland*
Producer: *New Midleton Distillery*
ABV: *40%* • **Bottle:** *70 cl*

Typology: *Single pot still Irish Whiskey*
Production: *double distillation in copper alembic stills.*

One of the main characteristics that differentiates Irish and Scotch whiskey is the style of Irish pure pot still whiskeys, which use a mixture of both malted and unmalted barley. So, what are the reasons behind this choice? In the first two decades of the 1800s, the high number of taxes imposed by the British Empire drastically reduced the number of legal distilleries to about twenty. Since taxation affected malted barley in particular, the distillers decided to include a portion of unmalted barley in the mash bill. The experiment was successful, given that the unmalted barley gave body and a particular spiciness to the distilled spirit. Green Spot is produced by the large New Midleton distillery and in the distant past was sold in the Dublin-based Mitchell grocery store, which was already buying it from Jameson at the beginning of the 20th century. Green Spot is a no-age-statement whiskey, although it contains whiskey that is aged 7-9 years, and is aged in a mix of 25% Sherry casks and 75% Bourbon casks.

Tasting
Nose: *grain, vanilla, tropical fruit*
Palate: *vanilla, toffee, mint, wood*
Finish: *pastry cream and spices*

Connemara 12

Features: *peated Irish whiskey.*

Country: *Ireland*
Producer: *Cooley Distillery*
ABV: *40%* • **Bottle:** *70 cl*

Typology: *Single Malt Irish Whiskey*
Production: *double distillation in copper alembic stills.*

The belief that all Irish whiskey is unpeated originates from its tormented history, which left few survivors before its rebirth. None of the brands produced by the New Midleton distillery used peat. It took the Teeling family two years to convert a disused potato alcohol plant into the Cooley Distillery, inaugurating it in 1987, and it played a part in the revival of whiskey on The Emerald Isle. The distillery is named after the peninsula and mountain range of the same name near County Louth. In 1992, it created its first Single Malt, Locke's, and in 2011 the distillery was bought by Beam, which later became Beam Suntory.

Connemara, named after the famous area in the Western region of County Galway, is one of the brands produced by the same distillery that makes Tyrconnel Single Malt and Greenore Single Grain, later renamed Kilbeggan Single Grain. Connemara 12 has very similar smoky and maritime characteristics to several of its Scottish island counterparts.

Tasting

Nose: *spices, aromatic herbs, citrus fruit, grains, smoke*
Palate: *lemon, creamy, notes of rhubarb and apple*
Finish: *dry, sweet and smoky*

CASK   ENGTH

WIDOW JANE
STRAIGHT BOURBON WHISKEY
AGED 10 YEARS IN AMERICAN OAK

PURE LIMESTONE MINERAL WATER
FROM THE WIDOW JANE MINE · ROSENDALE, NY

1090	148	2016
BARREL #	BOTTLE #	DATE

700ML   57% ALC/VOL (114 PROOF)

Widow Jane
Straight Bourbon

Features: *water, grains.*

Country: *USA*
Producer: *Widow Jane Distillery*
ABV: *45.5%* • **Bottle:** *70 cl*

Typology: *Straight Bourbon Whiskey*
Production: *discontinuous distillation in copper alembic stills.*

The distillery is situated in the post-industrial district of Red Hook, in the heart of Brooklyn, and curiously shares the property with Cacao Prieto, an organic chocolate factory, which happens to have the same owner. Production is based on the use of organic non-GMO grains, including Baby Jane corn, which the distillery created by cross-breeding a native barley species and Hopi Blue Mexican corn. Widow Jane was a famous mine in Rosendale, whose materials were used for the construction of iconic buildings such as the White House, the pedestal of the Statue of Liberty, the Brooklyn Bridge and the Empire State Building. The mine, whose original name was the Rosendale Limestone Mine, closed in 1970. Its owner A.J. Snyder had the reputation of being a despotic employer and an even crueler husband. His wife Jane, however, was well liked in the community and when her husband died everybody began referring to it as the Widow Jane Mine. The water used in the distillery's whiskey making comes from this very mine, and has an excellent mineral content thanks to its filtration by the limestone layers. The distillery has only been in operation since 2012, so only a part of its commercialized whiskey was produced on site. Widow Jane Straight Bourbon Whiskey is its best known product and is a 10-year-old Single Barrel bourbon that was distilled before the distillery opened, therefore sourced from another producer which is a very common practice in the United States.

Tasting
Nose: *citrus fruit, toffee, caramel, pastry cream*
Palate: *creamy, notes of cherries, wood, oranges, herbs and spices*
Finish: *crème brûlée, citrus fruit jelly and spices*

Koval Four Grain

Features: *organic grains, only single barrel, 114-liter (30-gallon) barrels.*

Country: *USA*
Producer: *Koval Distillery*
ABV: *47%* • **Bottle:** *50 cl*

Typology: *Single Barrel Whiskey*
Production: *discontinuous distillation in copper alembic stills.*

The Koval Distillery is in the northern suburbs of Chicago. Despite having only been founded in 2008, Koval has made a fundamental contribution to the overwhelming rise of craft distilling in America. The founders, husband and wife Robert and Sonat Birnecker, abandoned their academic careers to give life to Chicago's first distillery since the mid-1800s. They had a clear objective: to produce an organic whiskey without buying distilled spirits from other producers. It received extremely positive reviews and the project met with overwhelming success, confirmed by various awards. Robert Birnecker is one of the most experienced distillers in the United States, and has personally contributed to the training of over 2,500 aspiring distillers and the creation of about 100 craft distilleries in the U.S. and Canada.

Koval's whiskeys are unusual because they are all single barrel, aged for two to four years in 114-liter (30-gallon) new, charred American Minnesota oak barrels, in compliance with the Bourbon product specification. Each of the bottles identifies the barrel number from which it came, making it virtually possible to trace the entire history of the whiskey. It makes a Bourbon with an unusual mash bill of corn and millet, a 100% rye whiskey, a 100% rheat whiskey, two rare whiskeys with a mash bill of 100% millet and 100% oats respectively, and a 100% rye Moonshine whiskey.

The Four Grain whiskey, aged in small heavily charred 114-liter (30-gallon) barrels, is perhaps the distillery's most well-known creation, and is the only one of its whiskeys to use just malted grains (oats, malted barley, rye and wheat), giving the nod to the Scots.

Tasting
Nose: *banana, biscuit*
Palate: *vanilla, apple pie, creamy and spicy*
Finish: *wood, cinnamon*

SONOMA COUNTY

EST. 2010

DISTILLING CO.

2nd CHANCE · WHEAT

70 CL

DOUBLE ALEMBIC POT DISTILLED
ALCOHOL 49% BY VOLUME [98 PROOF]

Sonoma 2nd chance Wheat

Features: *mainly wheat grain, direct-fire alembic stills, gradual dilution, small barrels.*

Country: *USA*
Producer: *Sonoma County Distillery*
ABV: *47.1%* • **Bottle:** *70 cl*

Typology: *American Whiskey*
Production: *double distillation in discontinuous copper alembic stills.*

Like the adjacent Napa Valley, Sonoma is mainly famous for its vineyards. The founder of the distillery, Adam Spiegel, is convinced that the quality of his whiskey is largely due to the same climatic conditions that have made the area's wines so successful. The sea, which is only about 12 miles away, acts as a perfect balance between changes in temperature and humidity.

The distillery was founded in 2010, and for a while Spiegel received invaluable help and consultation from Hubert Germain Robin, a native of Cognac and, according to some, producer of the best brandy in California. The Cognac influence can be seen in the direct-fire discontinuous alembic stills of Portuguese and Spanish origin which, in addition to double distillation, have a much lower yield compared to more modern stills. Generally the whiskeys are aged in 57, 114 and 200-liter (15, 30 and 53-gallon) new charred barrels and then finished in "old wood" barrels. The French influence is found in the last stage before bottling: water is added very gradually to proof the whiskey down to a lower strength and thereby avoiding the final shock.

2nd Chance is made with a mash bill of unmalted wheat and malted rye. It is called "2nd Chance" because the rye and bourbon barrels are given a 'second chance' to age whiskey. The label in Europe does not mention the word "whiskey" because it does not meet the minimum aging requirement of three years.

Tasting
Nose: *caramel, spices, wood*
Palate: *grains, caramel, black pepper, lemon, toffee*
Finish: *caramel, raisins, spices*

Four Roses Single Barrel

Features: *uses 5 different yeasts and two unique mash bills.*

Country: *USA*
Producer: *Four Roses Distillery*
ABV: *50%* • **Bottle:** *70 cl*

Typology: *Bourbon Whiskey*
Production: *double distillation in copper alembic stills.*

Every Single Barrel whiskey produced by Four Roses can be a surprise. Four Roses is actually the only distillery that combines 5 proprietary yeast strains with two separate mash bills, one is 60% corn, and the other is 75% corn, to produce 10 distinct Bourbon recipes in the same plant. The yeasts are indicated with the letters V, K, O, Q and F, while A and B indicate the mash bills. The distillery's standard products are made with a combination of these recipes, while each Single Barrel whiskey contains just one type of Bourbon and for this reason it can be interesting to try them. Four Roses uses the combination of a column alembic still, in which the first distillation takes place to end up with about 66% ABV, and a pot still that purifies the distilled spirit and raises the alcohol content to about 70%.

Tasting
Nose: *caramel, vanilla, maple syrup*
Palate: *sweet with notes of caramel, mint*
Finish: *spicy and sweet*

MASTERSON'S

10-YEAR-OLD
STRAIGHT RYE WHISKEY

*Enshrined within, 100% rye
whiskey deemed to be as rare
as the man himself!*

Gambler, buffalo hunter, Army
scout, gunfighter and newspaperman, William "Bat" Masterson
did it all and did it well. And
what better way to honor such
a rarefied man than with a truly
exceptional whiskey. Crafted by
artisans, distilled in a pot still
and aged in white-oak casks for
just over 10 years, it's the kind
of drink that Bat would've surely

Masterson's 10 Years
Old Straight Rye

Features: *100% Rye grains.*

Country: *Canada*
Producer: *Alberta Distillery*
ABV: *45%* • **Bottle:** *70 cl*

Typology: *Straight Rye Whiskey*
Production: *discontinuous distillation in copper alembic stills.*

A bottle in honor of a rather atypical legendary character of the Wild West, William Barclay 'Bat' Masterson, who was a sheriff between the 19th and 20th centuries, spending his life on horseback capturing dangerous bandits, among other things. The label says "Gambler, buffalo hunter, army scout, gunfighter and newspaperman, William 'Bat' Masterson did it all and did it well."

The Masterson's brand belongs to the Deutsch family, an important wine producer based in the United States, however this whiskey was produced in Canada by the Alberta distillery in Calgary, which was founded in 1946. The distillery, specialized in the production of rye whiskey, supplies its distilled spirit to many U.S. and Canadian companies. This whiskey is produced with rye grain from the Pacific Northwest and is released in small batches.

Tasting
Nose: *toasted wood, peppercorn, grains, cocoa*
Palate: *tobacco, caramel, coconut, aromatic herbs*
Finish: *ginger, piquant and spicy*

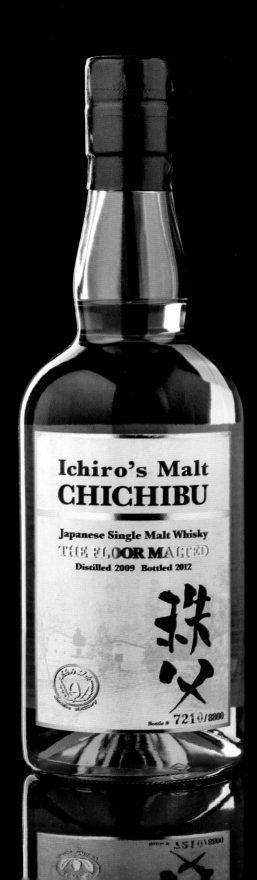

Chichibu
The Floor Malted

Features: *floor malted barley, long fermentation time.*

Country: *Japan*
Producer: *Chichibu Distillery*
ABV: *58.5%* • **Bottle:** *70 cl*

Typology: *Japanese Single Malt Whisky*
Production: *double distillation in copper alembic stills.*

The Chichibu distillery is near the town of the same name in the province of Saitama, about 62 miles west of Tokyo. The distillery is set in a woody mountainous area with extremely variable temperatures: winter is almost constantly below zero, while in summer it can often be above 30°C (86°F). These seasonal changes in temperature result in the increased expansion and contraction of the wood and the spirit volume, and guarantee an angels' share of 3/4% (about double that of Scotch whiskies), meaning that it matures very quickly. The Chichibu distillery has been operational since September 2008, and has had a great impact on the Japanese whisky market, immediately releasing high quality whiskies and also introducing notable innovations.

Chichibu is gradually turning into a self-sufficient distillery, having its own malting floor and using an increasing percentage of local barley, and part of its production is concentrated on peated whisky. Chichibu Floor Malted is made with the distillery's own malted barley, and is a limited release that indicates both the distillation year and the bottling date. Only 8,800 bottles of the 2009 edition were produced, bottled at 50.5% ABV.

Tasting
Nose: *vanilla, honey, pears, apples, spices*
Palate: *grains, biscuits, custard, vanilla and spices*
Finish: *citrus fruit, grains and spices*

Eddu Silver

Features: *uses pseudograins, direct-fire alembic stills, French oak casks.*

Country: *France*
Producer: *Distillerie des Menhirs*
ABV: *58.5%* • **Bottle:** *70 cl*

Typology: *Single Grain Whisky*
Production: *double distillation in copper direct-fire alembic stills.*

The Distillerie des Menhirs, situated in the heart of Brittany, was founded in 1986, and initially produced cider and Lambig, an apple brandy obtained from the distillation of cider. It started producing whisky about ten years later, and the first one was bottled in 2002. The whisky is distilled twice in direct-fire discontinuous stills and then aged in French oak casks.

Eddu Silver is made with 100% buckwheat, of which 20% is malted. In fact, Eddu means "buckwheat" in Breton and the distillery has become well-known for using this pure pseudograin, which is a non-graminaceous plant that belongs to the family Poligonaceae.

Tasting
Nose: *flowers, vanilla, nuts*
Palate: *vanilla, wood, notes of nuts*
Finish: *spices and wood*

Slyrs Single Malt

Features: *local barley, malt dried with beechwood, uses new barrels.*

Country: *Germany*
Producer: *Slyrs*
ABV: *43%* • **Bottle:** *70 cl*

Typology: *Single Malt Whisky*
Production: *distillation in copper alembic stills.*

The Bavarian Lantenhammera Schliersee distillery in Bavaria was founded in 1928, mainly producing brandy until 1999, which is when whisky began to become more popular. It was renamed Slyrs in 2003. The malt, produced with a local Bavarian barley, is produced at the Weyermann malting plant in the Bamberger Spezialmälzerei and dried over a beechwood fire, giving it spicy notes. Distillation takes place in a 1514-liter (400-gallon) alembic still. The distillery proudly promotes the purity of its water, which flows from the Bannwaldquelle spring in the Schliersee Alps.

This young Single Malt whisky rests for more than three years in American oak barrels: they are new barrels which are still very active, speeding up the aging process.

Tasting

Nose: *grain, vanilla*
Palate: *cereal grain biscuits, fruit, vanilla*
Finish: *spicy and toasted*

Mashing, Fermentation and Distillation

Tormore 16

anCnoc 12

Auchentoshan Virgin Oak

Springbank 10

Girvan Patent Still N° 4 Apps

Lagavulin 12 2017

Glenfarclas 15

Nikka Coffey Malt

Yoichi Single Malt

Glann Ar Mor Single Malt

The grains, stored in large silos, are ground and then transported in a large tank called a "mash tun". The ground grain, combined with hot water to extract the sugars, is mixed by huge blades that turn inside the mash tun. The sweet wort that is produced percolates down to the bottom of the mash tun. It is then cooled and moved into the washback, where fermentation takes place. The added yeasts convert the fermentable sugars in the wort into alcohol, producing a beer-like liquid called "wash", which has a 5-10% alcohol content. This is then distilled. The main purpose of distilling is to remove most of the water in the wash and concentrate the alcohol. There is a very simple concept behind this: the boiling point of alcohol is lower than that of water and therefore it starts to evaporate first. The alcoholic liquid is therefore heated and the alcohol vapors that rise are cooled and condensed back into liquid form. The "pot" that is used for this process is the alembic still. The traditional alembic still is called "pot still" or "discontinuous still", because it has to be filled and drained for each distillation. The shape of this kind of still is fairly important: tall pot stills with a narrow neck will produce lighter spirits – the most famous example is Glenmorangie – whereas wider alembic stills promote the vapors to rise and produce a more intense and oily spirit, like Lagavulin. The use of copper in the manufacturing of stills – on top of its malleability – is down to its organoleptic properties: during distillation, copper reacts with the distillate and eliminates impurities and unpleasant compounds, i.e. sulphur. With a continuous column alembic still, introduced in the 19th century, the mash enters the columns continuously, without it having to be drained each time. The column contains perforated plates that set up chambers within the still, and the distillate becomes lighter and lighter as it passes through each level. Therefore the height of the column and number of plates, in addition to other factors related to the number of columns and type of construction technology, affect the end spirit. Distillation methods are not categorized by which still is used – pot still or column still – but by whether the distillation process is discontinuous or continuous, as they produce completely different types of spirits. There are hundreds of variations of alembic stills for both continuous and discontinuous distillation.

Tormore 16

Features: *alembic stills fitted with a purifier.*

Country: *Scotland (Speyside)*
Producer: *Tormore Distillery*
ABV: *48%* • **Bottle:** *70 cl*

Typology: *Single Malt Scotch Whisky*
Production: *double distillation in copper alembic stills.*

Tormore was founded in 1958, and its main function, like all Single Malt whisky distilleries up until a few years ago, was to supply malt for the famous Long John blended whisky. It was only recently that it started releasing Single Malt whiskies on the market on a regular basis. The distillery's architecture is quite unique: designed by famous architect Sir Albert Richardson, it has a distinctive green roof and the same color is picked out on the buildings. Some have compared it to a power plant or even described it as looking like a hotel. The founder, Lewis Rosenstiel, was a controversial figure, although his ties with the American mafia and bosses Frank Costello and Meyer Lanski were only established after his death.

One of the distillery's distinctive characteristics is that it has purifiers attached to its stills – something it has in common with Glen Grant – which only allow the lighter part of the spirit to exit, while the heavier vapors are retained inside the alembic still to be redistilled. This device produces a lighter and cleaner spirit, as the name of the system suggests.

The 16-year-old whisky, released in 2014, ages in Bourbon barrels and is bottled without chill-filtration or artificial coloring. It is produced in small batches, which are specified on the label, and aging takes place in American white oak barrels.

Tasting

Nose: *biscuit, vanilla, white fruit*
Palate: *spices, orange peel, white fruit*
Finish: *sweet and spicy with notes of pastry cream*

anCnoc

12 YEARS OLD

anCnoc

HIGHLAND SINGLE MALT
SCOTCH WHISKY

PRONOUNCED: [*a-nock*]

The Knockdhu Distillery is situated
beneath the black knock hill, known to
the locals by its Gaelic name of anCnoc

DISTILLED, MATURED AND BOTTLED IN
SCOTLAND BY THE KNOCKDHU DISTILLERY
COMPANY, ABERDEENSHIRE, AB54 7LJ.

Established 1894

70cle 40%vol.

anCnoc 12

Features: *worm tubs to cool the vapors during distillation.*

Country: *Scotland (Highlands)*
Producer: *Knockdhu Distillery*
ABV: *40%* • **Bottle:** *70 cl*

Typology: *Single Malt Scotch Whisky*
Production: *double distillation in copper alembic stills.*

The anCnoc brand comes from the Knockdhu distillery – Knockdhu means Black Hill in Gaelic – founded in 1893, and although it wasn't particularly well-known until a few years ago, it played an important part in the history of Scotch whisky. It was the first and only distillery built by the Distillery Company Limited (DCL) which, after several acquisitions and mergers, evolved into today's drink giant, Diageo. The DCL was an amalgamation of six major grain whisky distilleries which in 1877 controlled 75% of whisky production. They chose Knock as the ideal place to open the distillery because of its vicinity to springs, barley fields and peat bogs, as well as the nearby railroad. However, it suffered the same fate as many other distilleries, opening and closing over the years. In 1972, it abandoned direct-fire alembic stills for stills that are heated by steam. In 1983, it was one of the many distilleries that fell victim to the Whisky Loch. Knockdhu only released their first Single Malt in 1990, which was renamed anCnoc in 1993 to avoid confusion with Knockando. Although it still produces whisky that is almost entirely handmade, Knockdhu is a model distillery in terms of energy consumption and respect for the environment. The distillery has developed an external ecological effluent treatment system for its wastewater, which removes the copper from the water through phytoremediation. Its historical importance is also given to the fact that it is one of the few distilleries that still uses worm tubs rather than modern condensers to condense the vapors produced during distillation. The name of these tubs derives from their snake-like shape, and they are immersed in large tanks of cold water that are outside the distillery. anCnoc 12 is the result of the balanced assembly of Bourbon casks.

Tasting
Nose: *grain, honey, flowers, biscuit*
Palate: *weet, spicy, honey with a note of lemon and apples*
Finish: *notes of grain, biscuit*

THE TRIPLE DISTILLED
AUCHENTOSHAN
SINGLE MALT SCOTCH WHISKY

VIRGIN OAK
LIMITED RELEASE

To preserve our triple distilled non chill-filtered spirit in **Virgin Oak** - when convention insists on finest bourbon or sherry casks? The answer lies in smooth **chocolate cream**, spiced orange and toasted vanilla.

EVERY SINGLE DROP TRIPLE DISTILLED | 700ml e | 46%alc./vol.

BATCH TWO

AUCHENTOSHAN
DISTILLERY

Auchentoshan
Virgin Oak

Features: *triple distillation, aged in new barrels.*

Country: *Scotland (Lowlands)*
Producer: *Auchentoshan Distillery*
ABV: *40%* • **Bottle:** *70 cl*

Typology: *Single Malt Scotch Whisky*
Production: *triple distillation in copper alembic stills.*

The Auchentoshan distillery, founded in 1823 and now almost incorporated into the suburbs of Glasgow, has a beautiful visitors center that is visited by numerous tourists and enthusiasts every year. The visit is a unique experience because the distillery has a very unusual characteristic: it is the only Scottish distillery to triple distil all is products. Triple distillation produces a new make spirit with an average alcohol content of 81% (compared to the about 70% obtained through double distillation) and a "cleaner" aromatic profile that highlights the notes of malt, fruit and citrus fruit, which give Auchentoshan whisky its extreme smoothness.

The distillery was founded by John Bulloch under the name Duntocher, along the banks of the river Clyde. As with many "early" distilleries, the project quickly went bankrupt and then passed through the hands of several owners.

In addition to its triple distillation, Auchentoshan Virgin Oak is also aged in "virgin" barrels, made of new wood, which yield aromatic substances faster than used barrels, accelerating the aging process.

Tasting
Nose: *vanilla, nutmeg, spices*
Palate: *vanilla, coconut, orange*
Finish: *sugar, vanilla, spices*

Springbank 10

Features: *one of the stills uses direct-fire, distilled two and half times, entire production process performed on site using floor malted barley.*

Country: *Scotland (Speyside)*
Producer: *Springbank Distillery*
ABV: *46%* • **Bottle:** *70 cl*

Typology: *Single Malt Scotch Whisky*
Production: *distilled two and half times in copper alembic stills.*

The Springbank distillery, founded in 1898, undoubtedly best represents the history and tradition of whisky distilling in the 1900s. All three brands (Hazelburn, Springbank and Longrow) use malt produced on the distillery's malting floors for their entire production, and the workers alternate between malting and distillation (as well as working at the nearby Glengyle distillery). The wash stills, used for the first distillation, are still heated with direct fire from beneath, and the entire production process is carried out manually. The Mitchell family play an important role in the area, employing dozens of people in their two distilleries and the historic Cadenhead's, an independent bottler, also owned by the family.

The distillery creates three types of whisky with three different names: in addition to Springbank (12-15ppm), which is distilled two and half times, there are two other brands, Hazelburn, an unpeated triple-distilled whisky, and Longrow, a very peaty twice-distilled whisky (50-55ppm), both named after closed distilleries in the area.

The Springbank malt whisky is created by exposing malted barley to 6 hours of peat smoke and 30 hours of neutral warm air. The "two and a half times" distillation process is performed with three stills, also used for triple distillation, with parts of the spirit going through distillation twice and some parts three times.

Tasting
Nose: *grain, wood, vanilla*
Palate: *nuts, vanilla, ginger, smoke*
Finish: *dry, smoky, cocoa*

THE GIRVAN PATENT STILL

SINGLE GRAIN SCOTCH WHISKY

In 1963 our first Girvan Patent
Still ran with spirit. Almost
three decades later in 1992 we
installed a pioneering new still
which we named "No. 4 Apps" –
a distillery term for "apparatus".

No.4
APPS

This unique still, operated under a
vacuum, permits distillation at low
temperatures. Delivering a pure,
vibrant and fruity single grain spirit,
ripe for maturation in our vanilla-
rich American Oak.

42% vol
42% alc/vol

WILLIAM GRANT & SONS
INDEPENDENT FAMILY DISTILLERS SINCE 1887

70cl ℮
700ml

DELICIOUSLY DIFFERENT

Notes of candied fruit and cream,
balanced by oak. It is, quite simply,
Deliciously Different single grain whisky.

Approved by Master Distiller

Girvan Patent Still
N° 4 Apps

Features: *Single grain distilled from two multi-pressure stills.*

Country: *Scotland*
Producer: *Girvan Distillery*
ABV: *42%* • **Bottle:** *70 cl*

Typology: *Single Grain Scotch Whisky*
Production: *continuous distillation in multi-pressure stills.*

The Girvan distillery was founded in 1963, under the supervision of Charles Grant Gordon, and the first drop of distilled spirit saw the light after just nine months, symbolically on Christmas day. It is said that the decision to build the distillery was prompted by a diplomatic incident. The Grant family made a commercial to promote their product and DCL, which at the time supplied William Grant with grain whisky for his blend, took umbrage at this and decided to cut off supplies. This episode, together with the lack of grain whisky to make blended whiskies, could also be one of the reasons why Glenfiddich Pure Malt was released in the same year.

In 1992, the distillery underwent major renovations and technological upgrades, and the original alembic stills were replaced by more efficient multi-pressure stills that operate under a vacuum, with capacity to produce 25 million gallons of anhydrous alcohol a year. The Girvan distillery also has the stills to produce Hendrick's gin, and between 1968 and 1975 it also distilled Ladyburn Single Malt whisky.

The Girvan Patent Still series was released in 2014, after a few previous shy attempts. The Girvan Patent Still N° 4 Apps takes its name from Apparatus number 4 which was in the distillery until 1992, when it was renovated.

Tasting
Nose: *fruit and vanilla*
Palate: *candied fruit, candy floss, vanilla*
Finish: *sweet and smooth*

Lagavulin 12 2017

Features: *shape of the alembic stills,*
bottled at natural cask strength.

Country: *Scotland* **Typology:** *Single Malt Scotch Whisky*
Producer: *Lagavulin Distillery* **Production:** *double distillation in copper*
ABV: *42%* • **Bottle:** *70 cl* *alembic stills.*

Lagavulin celebrated its 200th anniversary in 2016, and is one of the famous distilleries in the south of Islay, situated halfway between Ardbeg and Laphroaig. It is undoubtedly one of the most famous Single Malt distilleries in the world, thanks to its quality and also to the introduction of the Classic Malt collection in 1988, which was a success from day one. Lagavulin malt whisky has been a fundamental part of the White Horse blend for a long time. The creator of White Horse, Peter Mackie, bought the distillery in 1889, and created the famous brand the following year. There used to be a second distillery, Malt Mill, where today's visitor center now stands, which was made famous by Ken Loach's film *The Angels' Share* and built by Mackie himself to take revenge against Laphroaig: for several decades the Mackies had acted as agents for the nearby Laphroaig, but in 1908 it decided to sell its product directly. Malt Mill closed in 1962.

Lagavulin's pear-shaped alembic stills, very short in relation to their width, promote the ascent of even the heaviest vapors and influences its character, which is strong and intense.

Lagavulin 12 Years Natural Cask Strength, bottled after aging without being diluted, has been released annually in a limited edition since 2002, and whereas the 16-year-old uses Sherry and Bourbon casks, this whisky is aged exclusively in Bourbon casks.

Tasting (2017)
Nose: *ash, smoke, citrus fruit, grass*
Palate: *salt, lemon, vanilla, custard*
Finish: *dry and maritime with toasted notes*

Glenfarclas 15

Features: *direct-fired alembic stills, mainly uses Sherry casks.*

Country: *Scotland*
Producer: *Glenfarclas Distillery*
ABV: *46%* • **Bottle:** *70 cl*

Typology: *Single Malt Scotch Whisky*
Production: *double distillation in copper alembic stills.*

Although officially the Glenfarclas distillery was founded in 1836, it is highly likely that it began distilling illegally long before. The first legal license was given to Robert Hay, who held it until his death in 1865. His neighbor, John Grant, bought it for £512 and the Grant family, now in its the sixth generation, still owns it.

Thanks to its independence from the logic of large companies and shareholders, the distillery still uses traditional methods, remaining faithful to practices that have almost totally fallen into disuse, like heating the stills with direct fire from beneath. Steam heating was introduced in 1981, but was later abandoned because the results were considered unsatisfactory. Heating with direct fire requires a special tool to prevent the liquid from sticking to the bottom of the still; this mechanism is called "rummager", which is a long copper chain that mechanically rotates around the base of the still like a giant whisk.

Glenfarclas was also one of the first distilleries to believe in tourism, opening its doors to visitors in 1973. Its propensity to manage stocks and its Single Malts, made it possible for the distillery to create the Family Casks collection, with vintages spanning five decades from the 1950s through to the 1990s. It mainly uses Sherry casks and the 15-year-old is a perfect representation of the distillery's spirit.

Tasting

Nose: *vinous, peppercorn, wood, red fruit, cocoa*
Palate: *orange peel, sultana, walnuts, chocolate, red fruit*
Finish: *nuts, spices, cocoa, tobacco*

Nikka Coffey Malt

Features: *made from malted barley distilled in column stills.*

Country: *Japan*
Producer: *Miyagikyo Distillery*
ABV: *45%* • **Bottle:** *70 cl*

Typology: *Japanese Single Grain Whisky*
Production: *continuous distillation in alembic stills.*

The history of the Coffey stills that produce this spirit starts in the 1960s, when Masataka Taketsuru realized that it was time to improve the level of quality in the art of blending by using "grain whisky" that was made the Scottish way. Up until then, Japanese blended whiskies were made with malt and industrial neutral alcohol. In 1964, the Nishinomiya distillery started using Coffey stills, and Black Nikka was launched in 1965. The Coffey stills are now housed in the Miyagikyo distillery in Miyagi prefecture, opened in 1969 to produce Single Malts. Until 2001, the distillery was called "Sendai", named after the city it is in, after which it assumed its current name. Sales collapsed in 1989, mainly due to the effects of the new taxation on alcohol, and Nikka used the opportunity to give its industrial operations a major overhaul. In 1998, the Coffey stills were moved from Nishinomiya to Miyagikyo, where they were put into operation the following year.

Nikka had been making malt whiskies in Coffey stills since the 1970s, but it only became a commercial product, Nikka Coffey Malt, in 2014. In Scotland you can't associate the word Malt with that of Coffey, as it is a still that permits continuous distillation: the regulation for Scotch whisky law establishes that only a malt whisky that is distilled in a pot still can be called "malt." If this whisky was distilled in Scotland, it would fall into the "single grain" category.

Tasting
Nose: *citrus fruit, vanilla, white fruit, candied fruit, black pepper*
Palate: *lemon, candied fruit, pastry cream, tropical fruit*
Finish: *fruity with notes of prunes, lemon and a hint of bitter herbs*

NIKKA WHISKY

SINGLE MALT
YOICHI

余市蒸溜所 シングルモルト
北海道 余市蒸溜所でつくられたモルト原酒

PRODUCED BY THE NIKKA WHISKY
DISTILLING CO.,LTD.,JAPAN

ウイスキー

alc.45% WHISKY

Yoichi Single Malt

Features: *uses direct coal-fired alembic stills.*

Country: *Japan*
Producer: *Yoichi Distillery*
ABV: *45%* • **Bottle:** *70 cl*

Typology: *Japanese Single Malt Whisky*
Production: *double distillation in copper alembic stills.*

The wanderlust father of Japanese whisky, Masataka Taketsuru, settled in his first stable home in 1934, when he left Kotobuyika Co and founded his company Dai Nippon Kaju. He chose Hokkaido for his new adventure, which he had always considered an area very similar to Scotland. By the end of the same year, the Yoichi distillery had been built on the banks of the river of the same name. At first it mainly used apples to produce juice and cider, products that could be sold immediately and therefore useful for financing the project. Unfortunately, the juice was not initially a success, considered too cloudy by consumers, and in 1936, Taketsuru used the excess stock and products rejected by customers to produce an apple brandy, and in the second half of the same year he started to make whisky.

The stills are still heated by a direct coal fire and attended to by a stoker, just like in the olden days. Economically this is a disadvantageous choice, but the distillery fully believes it is the right one, even standing by it when, in 2003, it had to install an expensive filter system to reduce environmental impact. Thanks to the distillery's fidelity to tradition, its choice to make lightly peated whisky and its location, some venture to say that Yoichi perfectly embodies the Scottish spirit. Due to the need to produce whisky to use in blends, Yoichi distills different types of whiskies that display either extremely delicate smoke or very heavy smoke. Yoichi Single Malt is a No-Age-Statement whisky and preserves the almost centenary identity of this unique distillery.

Tasting

Nose: *floral and maritime notes, peat, spices, ginger*
Palate: *spices, fruit, nuts, chocolate and smoke*
Finish: *long, ripe fruit, salt and a fresh maritime finish*

Glann Ar Mor
Single Malt

Features: *direct-fired alembic stills, worm tubs to cool the steam during distillation, slow distillation.*

Country: *France*
Producer: *Glann ar mor Distillery*
ABV: *46%* • **Bottle:** *70 cl*

Typology: *Single Malt Whisky*
Production: *double distillation in copper alembic stills.*

Glann Ar Mor, which in Gaelic means "by the sea", is the unpeated expression of the distillery from which it takes its name (the peated whisky is called "Kornog"). The distillery uses methods that have almost fallen into disuse, including direct-fire heating, extremely slow distillation and worm tubs to cool the steam during distillation. Aging takes place in warehouses facing the sea and all the products retain their natural color and are non-chill filtered.

The unpeated Single Malt is produced with the Maris Otter barley variety, commonly used in the past but almost completely abandoned since the 1990s, although it is still much appreciated for brewing. Maris Otter reinforces the primary notes of malt and for this it was widely used in traditional British beers, also because it grew well in the climate of the British Isles. The whisky is aged in Bourbon barrels.

Tasting
Nose: *biscuit, white fruit, syrupy fruit*
Palate: *sweet, creamy, white fruit, vanilla*
Finish: *grass, black tea, persistent*

Maturation and Bottling

Compass Box Spice Tree
Arran Amarone Cask Finish
Balblair 2005
Balvenie 12 Single Barrel
Glendronach 12 Years Old
Old Pulteney 12
Teeling Small Batch Irish Whiskey
Jack Daniel's Bottled in Bond Tennessee
Michter's US * 1 Small Batch Bourbon
Ichiro's Malt Mizunara Wood Reserve
Mackmyra Brukswhisky
Puni Vina
Lark Cask Strength Single Malt
Kavalan Bourbon Oak Matured

Although in some countries there are also spirits that are called whiskey even if they don't spend any time in a cask, generally whiskey passes a period of time in a barrel made of wood. When it leaves the alembic still, the whiskey can be anywhere between 70-90% ABV, depending on the type of distillation. It is generally diluted to about 62/64% ABV before being put into casks. Wood can be considered the fourth ingredient in whiskey, as the spirit generally develops most of its aromas, as well as its color, during cask maturation. It is roughly estimated that at least 70% of a whiskey's flavors and aromas are acquired during the maturation process. So why is it so important? Wood has different effects on the spirit during the maturation process. The first is a subtractive effect: the aromas of the white spirit, the new-make, are often rough and slightly angular, at times metallic, also due to the high alcohol content. Cask maturation softens, rounds, shapes or even eliminates these edges. When the whiskey is peated, the "strength" of the peat decreases over the years, and this is also due to its contact with the wood.

The second is an additive effect: the wood and – in the case of used barrels – the alcoholic beverages previously contained in it, generate strong smelling aromatic substances, as well as color.

American white oak, used for Bourbon, is rich in sweet compounds like vanillin, while the softer and more malleable European oak produces more tannins and spicy notes. How the wood is treated also has an effect: thanks to the cracks that form in the wood, a charred barrel, used for Bourbon, allows easier penetration by the spirit than a toasted one.

The third is an interactive effect: the spirit interacts with both the wood of the barrel and the external environment.

Evaporation is part of this interactive effect. The maturation process is greatly influenced by the environment in which it takes place, particularly by variations of temperature and humidity that effect the evaporation rate. Temperature can also change the volume: the hotter it is, the more the whiskey expands. A whisky matured in sub-tropical environments, like the Taiwanese Kavalan, will mature faster than a Scotch whisky. Generally, whiskey aging warehouses are not artificially air-conditioned: in Scotland the traditional dunnage warehouses, with only three rows of barrels and earthen floors, have a constant temperature that promotes slow maturation. But innovation has also arrived in this part of the whiskey-making process: the Michters distillery, for example, has decided to heat its warehouses in winter to reduce the temperature range.

The types of wood and barrels used for maturation have multiplied: the traditional, hogshead and butt barrels – respectively 200, 250 and 500 liters (53, 66 and 132 gallons) – have been joined by the quarter cask (125 liters – 33 gallons) and other different-sized barrels. Bourbon and Sherry casks are no longer the only alternatives. Old wine barrels are also being used. Arran, for example, finishes its whiskey in Amarone casks for a few months, and the Italian distillery Puni uses Marsala barrels. The European oak is also no longer the only type of oak used. Mackmyra, for example, uses Swedish oak, while Ichiro Akuto has chosen one of the rarest varieties for his creations, Japanese Mizunara oak.

All that remains now is to bottle the whiskey, and there are two different ways to do this. The first is to follow a recipe and assemble the contents of lots of different barrels to obtain large quantities of the product, with similar characteristics between one batch and another. The second is to bottle small batches, or even a single barrel, limiting the number of bottles to a few hundred and obtaining a unique and unrepeatable whiskey.

Whiskey can be bottled at a chosen proof, for example 46%, by adding water, or at natural barrel strength without being diluted (the so-called "cask strength whiskey"). To prevent the whiskey from becoming cloudy when water or ice is added, many distillers chill-filter their whiskey to eliminate most of the oily substances. When a whiskey is not filtered, it is often labelled "not chill-filtered" or "non chill-filtered."

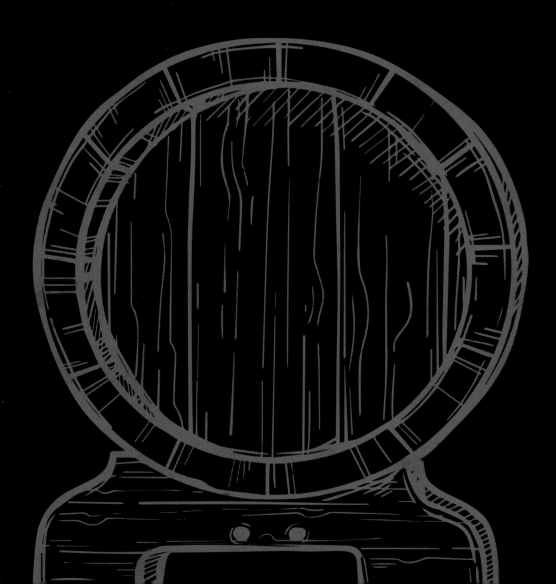

Compass Box Spice Tree

Features: *uses barrels made from different types of wood.*

Country: *Scotland*
Producer: *Compass Box*
ABV: *46%*
Bottle: *70 cl*

Typology: *Blended Malt Scotch Whisky*
Production: *double distillation in copper alembic stills from three distilleries.*

Compass Box, founded by John Glaser, is a fairly new producer of high quality Blended whisky. The market success of this new brand certainly took a lot of courage, but also an innovative approach. There is innovation in all his creations and this has also caused a few problems due to the strict rules for Scotch whisky. The first release of Just the Spice Tree used a maturation process that was then rejected, because it used special barrels with added wood elements that were not considered an integral part of the barrel. After being withdrawn from the market for a while, the product was released again, this time using custom-made casks with French oak for the heads and American oak for the bodies.

Spice Tree is a blended malt, whose recipe therefore only contains malt whisky. Another of Glaser's innovative ideas was to be 100% transparent about the components on the label. This was also rejected by the Scotch Whisky Association, as it could mislead the consumer on the actual age of the spirit. In any case, Glaser decided to make the information easily accessible and available on the company's website. Spice Tree is a blend of 20% Teaninich Single Malt, 20% Dailuaine and 60% Clynelish.

Tasting
Nose: *spices, vanilla, caramel, aromatic herbs*
Palate: *biscuit, ginger, vanilla, spices*
Finish: *spicy*

Arran
Amarone Cask Finish

Features: *secondary maturation in wine barrels.*

Country: *Scotland (Highlands/Islands)*
Producer: *Arran Distillery*
ABV: *50%* • **Bottle:** *70 cl*

Typology: *Single Malt Scotch Whisky*
Production: *double distillation in copper alembic stills.*

The Isle of Arran distillery, founded in 1995, was the first of the numerous distilleries that have opened in Scotland over the past few decades. The distillery is based in Lochranza, capital of the homonymous island of Arran (the southernmost of the Scottish islands). In the past there were numerous clandestine distilleries on the island, but only one legal one, Lagg, which was operational from 1825 to 1837.

When Harold Currie – former general manager of Chivas Brothers – set up a consortium to open a distillery on the island, he chose Lochranza, in the northern half of Arran, for its excellent and abundant water, as well as for its popularity with tourists. In fact, although it is still one of the smallest distilleries in Scotland, it has over 60,000 visitors a year.

Since 2004, Isle of Arran has only distilled a small percentage of peated malt whiskies: 10% at 20ppm and a further 5% at a much heavier 50ppm.

On the Amarone Barrel Finish label, the word finish" indicates double maturation: the whisky is first matured in Bourbon casks and then transferred to Amarone casks for a few months until it has finished maturing. This expression is bottled at 50% ABV, retains its natural color and is non-chill filtered. It is a "no age statement" whisky, which on the market is indicated with the acronym NAS.

Tasting
Nose: *black cherry, spices, wood, chocolate*
Palate: *black cherry, vanilla, spices, nuts*
Finish: *nuts, chocolate, spices*

Balblair 2005

Features: *bottled by vintage.*

Country: *Scotland (Highlands)*
Producer: *Balblair Distillery*
ABV: *46%* • **Bottle:** *70 cl*

Typology: *Single Malt Scotch Whisky*
Production: *double distillation in copper alembic stills.*

The first distillery was built in the village of Edderton in 1790, by James McKeddy. After a few months he was forced to move the ownership onto the Ross family, which ran it for over a century. In 1895, production was moved to a new location that was closer to the new railway line, although it continued using the same water source.

Like many other distilleries, the collapse of the Scotch industry in the early 1900s forced the distillery to close. Activities only resumed after the Second World War, when Churchill's edict imposed the reopening of many distilleries to produce whisky to be sold in particular to the Americans. In 1996, the distillery was purchased by Inver House Distillers Limited, now part of the Thai International Beverage Holdings group. Up until a few years ago, the distillery only produced a few Single Malt selections, and then it began bottling whisky that indicated the distillation year rather than the number of years it had been aged. In 2012, the distillery was used as one of the shooting locations for Ken Loach's film *The Angels' Share*.

This Balblair, distilled in 2005 and bottled in 2017, was matured in American white oak Bourbon casks. This method brings out the spirit's traditional fruity character, in particular the aromas of tropical fruit. Its character owes much to the long fermentation time, and the small stills give great structure to the whisky, also making it suitable for long periods of maturation. The design on the bottle is inspired by the Pictish symbols carved on a nearby standing stone called "Clach Biorach", which dates back to around 4000 years ago.

Tasting 2005 1st Release
Nose: *tropical fruit, spices, honey, green apple, citrus fruit and flowers*
Palate: *lemon, vanilla, yellow fruit*
Finish: *spices, white fruit, vanilla*

ESTᴰ 1892

SINGLE MALT SCOTCH WHISKY

Distilled at

THE BALVENIE®

Distillery, Banffshire
SCOTLAND

SINGLE BARREL

Cask Type *FIRST FILL*

AGED **12** YEARS

THIS BOTTLE IS ONE OF NO MORE THAN 300
DRAWN FROM A SINGLE CASK

CASK NUMBER	BOTTLE NUMBER
4775	16

7cl/700ml

THE BALVENIE DISTILLERY COMPANY
BALVENIE MALTINGS, DUFFTOWN,
BANFFSHIRE, SCOTLAND AB55 4BB

47.8%vol 47.8% alc./vol.

Balvenie 12
Single Barrel

Features: *single barrel, matured in first fill Bourbon barrels, floor malting.*

Country: *Scotland (Speyside)*
Producer: *Balvenie Distillery*
ABV: *47.8%* • **Bottle:** *70 cl*

Typology: *Single Malt Scotch Whisky*
Production: *double distillation in copper alembic stills.*

Balvenie is one of the most popular distilleries among enthusiasts, and not just for its whisky. The setting is stunning, with a series of buildings that develop around the railway and behind its majestic sister distillery Glenfiddich. Balvenie still practices floor malting to cover about 15% of its needs, using barley from the fields on its land, making it a distillery, at least partially, with an agricultural heart. A visit to Balvenie, available by appointment only, is one of the most beautiful in Scotland. Balvenie's sales have more than tripled in just a few years, becoming one of the top ten most sold Single Malt whiskies in the world. It has now increased production up to seven million liters (just over one and a half million gallons).

The distinctive characteristic of this 12-year-old is that it's a Single Barrel and therefore has not been assembled. Each first fill Bourbon barrel, i.e. used just once for Bourbon, produces a maximum of 300 bottles. Balvenie keeps the product constantly on the market, and tasting two products from the same distillery that have been aged for the same amount of time, using the same type of wood, and yet a single barrel expression, is a truly unique and highly educational experience. No two barrels are the same.

Tasting

Nose: *vanilla, custard, coconut, spices, yellow fruit, toasted wood*
Palate: *custard, lemon, yellow fruit, vanilla*
Finish: *yellow fruit, spices, tropical fruit*

Glendronach
12 Years Old

Features: *uses Sherry casks.*

Country: *Scotland (Highlands)*
Producer: *Glendronach Distillery*
ABV: *43%* • **Bottle:** *70 cl*

Typology: *Single Malt Scotch Whisky*
Production: *double distillation in copper alembic stills.*

The Glendronach distillery is located at the far eastern point of the Speyside region and has always stood out for its prevalent use of Sherry casks. It was founded in 1826, by a group of local farmers headed by James Allardice, and it was Scotland's second distillery to be licensed under the new Excise Act of 1823. After it was bought by William Teacher & Sons Ltd in 1966-1967, the coal-fired stills increased from 2 to 4. The coal (together with the peat) was also used in the malting process to dry the barley. Up until 1996, when the malting floor was discontinued, Glendronach whiskies were lightly peated to about 14ppm. The last legacy of this process, direct-fire heating, was removed and replaced by steam in 2005, but there are still many barrels in the distillery's warehouses that were produced with the old systems.

The abundant use of Sherry casks – this 12-year-old was matured in a combination of Oloroso Sherry and Pedro Ximenez casks – has made the distillery a reference point for lovers of this type of maturation, very widespread in the past but now little used due the high cost of the casks.

Tasting
Nose: *panettone, red fruit, cocoa, leather*
Palate: *red fruit, spices, candied fruit*
Finish: *nuts, chocolate, tobacco*

EST 1826 · WICK · SCOTLAND

OLD PULTENEY

SINGLE MALT SCOTCH WHISKY

ROBUST, WITH A DELICATE HINT OF SEA AIR

70cle   PRODUCED BY DISTILLERY MANAGER
40%vol
DISTILLED, MATURED AND BOTTLED IN SCOTLAND KW1 5BA

AGED
12
YEARS

Old Pulteney 12

Features: *worm tubs to cool the steam during distillation, whiskey with maritime notes and without peat.*

Country: *Scotland (Highlands)*
Producer: *Pulteney Distillery*
ABV: *40%* • **Bottle:** *70 cl*

Typology: *Single Malt Scotch Whisky*
Production: *double distillation in copper alembic stills.*

The Pulteney distillery was founded in 1826 and is named after Sir. William Pulteney, who at the beginning of the 19th century built a village with a large fishing port, helped by Thomas Telford, a civil engineer who was well-known for designing bridges, canals and aqueducts. The new settlement provided work for many of the peasants who had been kicked off their land during the Highland Clearances, and for a long time it was the most important herring fishing port in Scotland, with 800 fishing boats. The distillery is completely incorporated into the urban fabric of Wick, a name that replaced the previous one of Pulteneytown. Pulteney has two distinctive characteristics. The first is the curious shape of the wash still, which has an almost spherical upper lobe and the upper part terminating with a flat plate. The story goes that when the still arrived it had a swan neck, but this prevented it fitting into the small still room, so the top was simply cut off. The second is the use of worm tubs to cool the steam. The 12-year-old is matured in Bourbon casks and expresses a unique maritime character – something it has in common with Clynelish – so much so that it is described on the labels as being *The Maritime Malt*. Don't expect the same maritime notes of many peated whiskies of the islands; they are more reminiscent of the smell of sea air. Another distinctive characteristic of Pulteney whiskies, and in particular of this 10-year-old, are the notes of pears and apples.

Tasting

Nose: *flowers, pear, conifers, sea breeze*
Palate: *sweet, white fruit and sapidity*
Finish: *dry with maritime notes and hints of nuts*

Teeling Small Batch Irish Whiskey

Features: *matured in rum casks.*

Country: *Ireland*
Producer: *Teeling Distillery*
ABV: *40%*
Bottle: *70 cl*

Typology: *Irish Blended Whiskey*
Production: *blended whiskey double-distilled in copper alembic stills and a column alembic still.*

After opening the Cooley distillery in 1987 and selling it in 2011, the Teeling family continued to sell whiskey under the family name, using the Cooley's stock that was not part of the sale agreement.

At the same time, the family started two new projects: the first, in 2015, was a new distillery in the center of Dublin, the first operational distillery in the Irish capital in over 125 years; the second was buying the Great Northern Brewery in Dundalk, formerly owned by Diageo, and investing £35 million to convert it into the second largest distillery in Ireland after New Midleton. The distillery's label says "Since 1782" because this was the year that one of the family's ancestors, Walter Teeling, opened a distillery in Dublin.

Teeling Small Batch is a blended whiskey distilled in small batches. It retains its natural color, is non-chill filtered and contains a higher than usual ratio of malt to grain. It is finished in rum barrels for an additional 6 months.

Tasting

Nose: *vanilla, apple pie, red fruit, demerara sugar*
Palate: *vanilla, spices and grassy notes*
Finish: *grassy with notes of burnt sugar*

Jack Daniel's
Bottled in Bond Tennessee

Features: *Bottled-in-Bond whiskey.*

Country: *USA*
Producer: *Jack Daniel's Distillery*
ABV: *50%* • **Bottle:** *70 cl*

Typology: *Tennesee Whiskey*
Production: *distillation in column alembic stills.*

Jack Daniel's is one of the most iconic and well-known whiskeys in the world. Its fame has resulted in millions of gallons being produced and the creation of one of the most extensive sales networks in the business. After dominating the market almost unchallenged alongside other brands from the nearby Kentucky, changes at local level – with the advent of micro-distilleries – and global level – with sporadic research into new products – are changing scenarios, and Jack Daniel's has also had to start hunting for new consumers. One way to do this was to make a product using a little-known category of American whiskey, Bottled-in-Bond. Many of the brands on the market do not distill their own whiskey, buying it from distilleries that also produce whiskeys for "third parties", and therefore this category could be defined as being "operation transparency." In fact, the set of legal requirements say that a whiskey can only be defined as Bottled-in-Bond if the whiskey comes from a single distillery, is one distilling season and is distilled by one master distiller; it must be at least four years old and bottled at 100 proof (50% Vol). The Bottled-in-Bond Act was introduced in 1898, as a reaction to widespread adulteration in whiskey, and not only in the United States. One of the things that Jack Daniel's is most proud of is its Charcoal Mellowing process, which involves letting the whiskey slowly drip through 3 meters (10 ft) of hard sugar maple charcoal so it comes out with its distinctive smoothness.

Tasting
Nose: *caramel, banana, vanilla, toasted wood*
Palate: *vanilla, coconut, créme brulée, green apple, maple syrup*
Finish: *creamy with woody notes*

Michter's US *1
Small Batch Bourbon

Features: *aged in a heated warehouse, low barrel entry proof, unusual barrel finish.*

Country: *USA*
Producer: *Michetr's Distillery*
ABV: *50%* • **Bottle:** *70 cl*

Typology: *Bourbon Whiskey*
Production: *double distillation in column alembic stills and pot stills.*

The brand was founded in 1753, and the Magliocco family brought it back to life in the 1990s. For a long time it purchased spirits from other distilleries, providing the recipe and then maturing it themselves: the specification provided stated that they were to barrel the whiskey – the barrels are supplied by Michter's, at 103 proof (51.5% ABV instead of the usual 125 proof). In 2015, Magliocco inaugurated the new distillery with a beautiful pair of alembic stills: a 46-foot tall column still and a small pot still with a very unusual design. The maturation process was enriched with innovative aspects: first the barrels are toasted, using a "slow cooking" process that prepares the sugars that are present very deep in the wood, and then charred, because it is required by the product specification and is necessary to obtain the characteristic Bourbon and rye flavor. With this process the spirit penetrates the char layer and draws out the wood extractives. The new distillery also barrels the whiskey at 103 Proof. Finally, the warehouse is heated during the winter with a process called "heat cycling", which stimulates aging during the winter months. Michter's US *1 Small Batch Bourbon is made in small batches, indicated with a label on the neck of the bottle.

Tasting
Nose: *grain, nuts, vanilla*
Palate: *peppercorn, cinnamon, vanilla, maple syrup, raisins*
Finish: *spices and caramel with toasted notes*

Ichiro's Malt
Mizunara Wood Reserve

Features: *uses Mizunara oak casks.*

Country: *Japan*
Producer: *Ichiro Akuto*
ABV: *46%*
Bottle: *70 cl*

Typology: *Japanese Blended Malt Whisky*
Production: *double distillation in copper alembic stills, blend of two single malt whiskeys.*

Ichiro Akuto created this whisky by blending malts from his family's old Hanyu Distillery, shut-down in 2000, and the new Chichibu Distillery, and the result is an extremely special blended malt whisky. He also chose to use Mizunara oak casks, a rare variety specific to Japan.

Akuto's family began distilling whisky at the Hanyu Distillery in the 1980s, but it was closed less than two decades later due to the stock market crash. There were about 400 barrels of Hanyu left, which Ichiro uses for limited releases and also as an ingredient for blends like this.

Mizunara oak, or *Quercus mongolica*, is a type of wood that appeared in the whisky world thanks to the increase in Japanese whiskies. Its characteristics and very high cost makes it completely unsuitable for building barrels. The tree rarely grows straight, so it has to be seasoned outdoors and specially treated to straighten it. Moreover, the wood is very porous and prone to leaking because it possesses less tyloses than other types of wood, which effects the blockage of the vessels. The price to pay for unique flavors is therefore very high.

Chichibu also uses Mizunara fermentation vats and, in some cases, assemblies its whiskies in a large Mizunara vat over a period of at least 12 months.

Tasting
Nose: *lemon, honey, sandalwood, white grapes*
Palate: *spices, honey, white fruit, sandalwood*
Finish: *spicy, sweet*

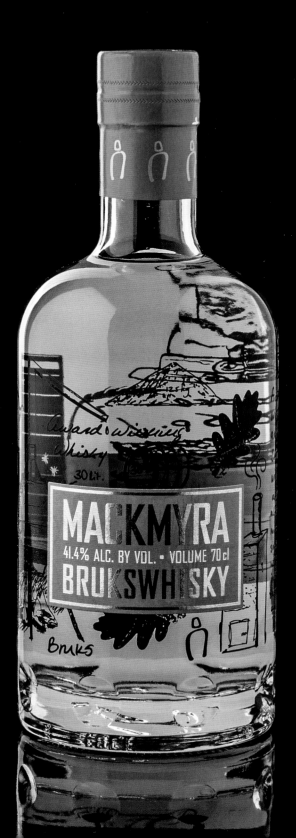

Mackmyra Brukswhisky

Features: *gravity distillery, uses Swedish oak casks.*

Country: *Sweden*
Producer: *Mackmyra Distillery*
ABV: *41.4%* • **Bottle:** *70 cl*

Typology: *Single Malt Whisky*
Production: *double distillation in copper alembic stills.*

It should come as no surprise that Sweden has whisky distilleries: the Swedes are extremely passionate about whisky and are among the most frequent visitors to Scottish distilleries, as well as having founded dozens of whisky clubs in their homeland. The Mackmyra project was born in 1998 and – after a few experimentations – the first distillery was built in 2002. On December 17th, 2011, a new Gravity distillery was inaugurated. The distillery uses stills that are the same size and shape as the previous ones, although they can be operated in three shifts. The old Mackmyra Bruk Distillery can produce 170,000 liters (37,000 gallons) of alcohol, which is used for experiments, while the gravity distillery produces about 500,000 liters (110,000 gallons). It is called a "gravity distillery" because the production process starts with feeding in the raw ingredients – malt, water and yeast – at the top, and then collects the new-make at the bottom. Biofuels are used throughout.

Mackmyra works with a concept that we could call a distributed distillery, as it matures its whisky in different areas of Sweden. It has even opened a Whisky Village in Gavle, north of Stockholm. There are numerous whiskies, some quite traditional – aged in Bourbon barrels – flanked by "Swedish" productions that use local oak barrels, similar to the French ones, and they are wood-smoked, using local tree species, rather than peat-smoked. Mackmyra Brukswhisky is an assembly of whiskies matured in first fill Bourbon, Sherry and Swedish oak casks, and it also contains a small portion of smoky whisky.

Tasting
Nose: *vanilla, pine needles, white fruit*
Palate: *red fruit, pastry cream and vanilla*
Finish: *baked apples, spicy with fresh notes of aromatic herbs*

Puni Vina

Features: *reaches full maturity in wine barrels, recipe contains three malted grains.*

Country: *Italy*
Producer: *Puni Distillery*
ABV: *43%* • **Bottle:** *70 cl*

Typology: *Malt Whisky*
Production: *double distillation in copper alembic stills.*

The Puni distillery, the only one in Italy based on a Scottish model, started production in 2012, thanks to the Ebensperger family. The modern and innovative building has a gridded pattern based on the ventilation slits that are typical of the brick barns in the area. All the main equipment is Scottish, while the five 12,000-liter (3000-gallon) fermentation vats are made from South Tyrolean larch and produced by a local company. The water comes from the town's water supply network, which uses a nearby water source. For the first few years, the distillery used three types of malt grains for the mash bill: barley, wheat and rye, the latter of which was grown in Val Venosta and malted in Germany. In the following years, it only produced barley malt whisky. In addition to this distinct blend of grains, the distillery has adopted two rather unusual practices: the first is to also use Marsala barrels for aging, to emphasize the whisky's Italian origins, while the second is using bunkers from the Second World War to mature part of the stock. Puni Vina encompasses all three of the distillery's unusual characteristics and is aged for five years in old Marsala barrels.

Tasting

Nose: *raisins, spices, nuts, dry biscuits*
Palate: *spices, white fruit, syrupy fruit and wild berries*
Finish: *spicy, cocoa, ripe fruit*

Lark Cask Strength
Single Malt

Features: *uses small barrels, local grains, bottled at natural cask strength, single barrel.*

Country: *Tasmania*
Producer: *Lark Distillery*
ABV: *58%* • **Bottle:** *50 cl*

Typology: *Single Malt Whisky*
Production: *double distillation in copper alembic stills.*

Bill Lark founded his distillery in 1992, obtaining the first distilling license issued in Tasmania in 153 years, and 150 years after the last active distillery closed. In addition to having paved the way for other distillers, he has also helped them to open by teaching them the trade, out of his own pocket. The distillery is located on a farm in Mount Pleasant, about 15 minutes from Hobart, where he found a group of investors who participated in the subsequent development of the distillery. Bill Lark says he had his moment of enlightenment during a trout fishing trip with his father-in-law. While sipping a glass of whisky, they realized they were surrounded by barley fields and abundant water sources and peat bogs. At that point, he wondered why there were no distillers in Tasmania. The whisky is mostly matured in 100-liter (22-gallon) barrels, and part of the barley is dried using local peat from the Brown Marsh Bog, which the distillery owns. His daughter Christy recently became the master distiller.

The whisky is a single cask expression, bottled at natural cask strength without being diluted. It is made with the Australian Franklin and Gairdner barley varieties.

Tasting
Nose: *spices, nuts, vanilla, honey*
Palate: *oily, notes of apples, vanilla, pastries and ginger*
Finish: *spicy with notes of orange and honey*

Kavalan Bourbon Oak Matured

Features: *matured in a tropical climate.*

Country: *Taiwan*
Producer: *Kavalan Distillery*
ABV: *46%* • **Bottle:** *70 cl*

Typology: *Single Malt Whisky*
Production: *double distillation in copper alembic stills.*

The Kavalan distillery was founded in 2005, partly to meet the needs of the country's whisky consumption, which is so high that it has made Taiwan one of the world's major whisky consumers. The numerous extensions that have been added to the distillery in just a few years are testimony to its success. The founder, entrepreneur Lee Tien Tsai, owner of King Car, had long dreamt of producing whisky, and when Taiwan joined the WTO in 2002, it gave him the impetus he needed to embark on this adventure. Located in the north-east of the country, it is in an area with significantly higher temperatures than Scotland. This is one of the reasons why the distilling method had to undergo some modifications, combining traditional condensers with another more efficient cooling system.

The warm and humid sub-tropical climate alone, with temperatures that often exceed 40°C (104°F), cause the whisky maturing in the barrels to evolve differently to those in Scotland, with an evaporation rate of over 10%, compared to the Scottish 1/2%. It therefore matures much faster and more aggressively, producing a whisky that already has fully-developed colors and flavors after just 3 years. The distillery very much focuses on maturing in old wine barrels, however Kavalan Bourbon Matured is the expression that truly encompasses this tropical soul, enhanced by the American oak.

Tasting
Nose: *vanilla, tropical fruit, nutmeg*
Palate: *mango, spices, coconut, banana*
Finish: *lemon and spices*

Serving and Tasting

As much as people try to lay down strict rules, whiskey is drunk and served in many different ways. There are also many different customs. In places where consumption is high and whiskey is considered a daily drink to enjoy in company, the glass it is served in is often of little importance, and it is served with many different things: for example, ice, water, soda, coke or lemonade. Elsewhere, where whiskey is considered a nectar to be drunk slowly, it has to be served in a tulip-shaped glass, with a glass of fresh water on the side to refresh the palate. None of the above is wrong, although it would be a bit silly to use an expensive single malt to make a whiskey and coke. There are dozens of technical tasting glasses for whiskey, none of which are perfect for all types of whiskey, but a Sherry glass is acceptable to start with. If you want to get to know the whiskey you're drinking, you have to start getting acquainted with it slowly. Swirl the whiskey around the glass, without turning the glass itself, coating its sides thoroughly. Then look at the legs that have formed and watch how quickly they run back down the sides. Bring the glass up to your nose and move it quickly from one nostril to the other. Then keep the glass under your nose for a few more seconds. Try to smell it with your mouth open. Now take a small sip to get used to the alcohol. Take a second sip, and this time keep it in your mouth a few seconds longer before swallowing it, making sure that it touches every part of the mouth.

Now swallow it. The back-nasal smell is important. On contact with the mouth, the alcohol fumes rise inside the nose, making it possible to perceive additional aromas.

Although many people are reluctant to add water to whiskey, it can be used to refresh the palate between one sip and another, or added, in varying quantities, directly to the glass. From a purely technical point of view, the addition of water is essential to understanding the merits and defects of a whiskey. Those who work in the world of whiskey, like blenders, mainly use their olfactory senses. They add the water to the whiskey gradually until it is diluted to 50%. But why do they do this? The chemical reaction when adding water to whiskey, reduces the alcohol content and raises the temperature slightly. This releases many of the flavors that are "imprisoned" in the whiskey so that they can be identified. Even just a few drops of water can facilitate this reaction. Water can also be useful to dilute the whiskey if it is being drunk with food.

Does adding water makes whiskey easier to drink? The reduced alcohol content certainly helps, but other factors must also be considered. Alcohol is a "smooth", sweet substance and diluting it makes it less concentrated. If "hard" flavors in a whiskey, for example tannins and spices, are not counterbalanced by alcohol, they will be much more evident.

Cocktails

Blood
& Sand

La Manica

Herbs
Manhattan

Manhattan

Hey Johnny
say Cheese

Milano
Whisky
Crusta

L'Amico
del Conte

Mint
Julep

Old
Fashioned

 Smook
Bloody

 Rob
il Saggio

 Sol
Levante

 Saving
Grace

 Tyrannie
Whisky

 Sazerac

Blood & Sand

Ingredients

4.3 cl (1.5 fl oz) Springbank 10
2.1 cl (0.75 fl oz) Punt & Mes
1.5 cl (0.5 fl oz) Sangue Morlacco liqueur
2.1 cl (0.75 fl oz) fresh orange juice

Method: shake • Glass: coupe glass
Garnish: cherries

Preparation

Put all the ingredients in a shaker, fill with ice and shake vigorously. Strain into a cocktail coupe glass and garnish with a maraschino cherry.

Herbs Manhattan

Ingredients

4.3 cl (1.5 fl oz) Masterson's 10 Years Old Straight Rye
4.3 cl (1.5 fl oz) Cocchi Storico Vermouth Torino
1 spoon Fernet
1.5 spoons Branca Menta
0.5 spoon Green Absinthe

Method: stir • Glass: Martini glass
Garnish: lemon twist (then discarded)*, a mint sprig

Preparation

Put all of the ingredients in a mixing glass and chill by leaving the mixture to partially dilute. Strain into a chilled cocktail glass and fragrance with a slice of lemon twist.

"Discarded" lemon twist means that you use the peel to spray the essential oil into the drink, but the zest itself is not used as a garnish.

Hey Johnny say Cheese

Ingredients

5 cl (1.75 fl oz) Ben Nevis 10
5 cl (1.75 fl oz) Rambutan-infused
3 cl (1 fl oz) Sweet potato puree
1 bar spoon cheese dip
2 dashes Tropical bitters
1.5 cl (0.5 fl oz) lime juice

Method and glass: shake, Japanese cup with lid
covered in embroidered fabric
Garnish: blue bow-tie pasta

Preparation

Put all the ingredients in a shaker, fill with ice and shake vigorously. Strain into the serving glass, which is also the garnish.

L'Amico del Conte

Ingredients

3.5 cl (1.25 fl oz) Sonoma
Wheat 2nd Chance
3 cl (1 fl oz)
Cocchi Americano
2.1 cl (0.75 fl oz)
Zucca Rabarbaro
2 dashes Angostura Bitters
2 dashes Orinoco Bitters

Method: stir
Glass: double rocks
Garnish: lemon twist

Preparation

Put all of the ingredients in a
mixing glass and chill by
leaving the mixture to dilute
thoroughly. Pour into an
extremely cold serving glass
and fill with ice cubes.
Fragrance and garnish with a
slice of lemon twist.

La Manica

Ingredients

3 cl (1 fl oz) Glenfarclas 15
0.75 cl (0.25 fl oz) Kornog
1.5 cl (0.5 fl oz) Marsala
3 cl (1 fl oz) Umeshu
2 dashes Angostura
Orange Bitters
4 dashes Angostura Bitters

Method: stir
Glass: Martini glass
Garnish: orange twist

Preparation

Put all the ingredients in a mixing
glass and leave to chill thoroughly.
Strain into a chilled cocktail glass,
fragrance and garnish with a slice
of orange twist.

Manhattan

Ingredients

4.3 cl (1.5 fl oz) Widow
Jane Rye
4.3 cl (1.5 fl oz) Red
Vermouth
4 dashes Bitters

Method: stir
Glass: Martini glass
Garnish: orange twist

Preparation

Put all of the ingredients in a
mixing glass, chill with ice and
dilute to taste. Strain into a chilled
cocktail glass and fragrance with
a slice of orange twist, which is
also to be used as a garnish.

Milano Whisky Crusta

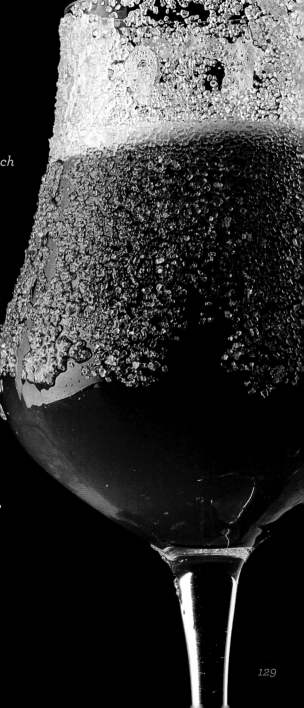

Ingredients

3.5 cl (1.25 fl oz) Teeling Small Batch
3 cl (1 fl oz) Fernet
1.5 cl (0.5 fl oz) Cointreau
0.75 cl (0.25 fl oz) lemon juice

Method: shake
Glass: tasting glass
Garnish: white sugar crust rim

Preparation

Roll a well-chilled tasting glass
in a container filled with sugar
until the entire surface is covered.
Put all the ingredients in a shaker,
fill with ice and shake vigorously.
Strain into the glass you prepared
beforehand.

Mint Julep

Ingredients

5 cl (1.75 fl oz) Jack Daniel's Bottled-in-Bond
5 dashes Bitters
15 g (0.5 oz) mint
15 g (0.5 oz) white sugar
Splash of soda

Method: build • Glass: cup
Garnish: mint sprig

Preparation

Put the sugar, bitters, mint and soda in the serving glass and muddle to dissolve the sugar and extract the aromas from the mint. Add the whiskey and a generous amount of crushed ice, then stir to melt the ice until you get the desired consistency. Garnish with crushed ice, red fruit and a large mint sprig. Drink through a Julep strainer so as not to wet your moustache!

Old Fashioned

Ingredients

5.7 cl (2 fl oz) Four Roses
Single Barrel
1 sugar cube
5 dashes Bitters
Splash of soda

Method: Build
Glass: double rocks
Garnish: orange twist
and one cherry

Preparation

Put the sugar cube in a mixing
glass and soak it with bitters to
taste. Add a splash of soda to
help dissolve it. Add the
whiskey, fill the glass with ice
cubes and stir until you get the
desired consistency. Garnish
with a slice of orange twist and
a maraschino cherry.

Rob il Saggio

Ingredients

5.7 cl (2 fl oz) Glenfarclas 15
2.1 cl (0.75 fl oz) Cocchi Storico
Vermouth
0.75 cl (0.25 fl oz) Carlo Alberto
Red Vermouth
Dash Orinoco Bitters

Method: stir
Glass: Martini glass

Preparation

Put all of the ingredients in a mixing
glass and leave to dilute a bit. Pour
into a chilled Martini glass, then
fragrance and garnish with a slice
of orange twist.

Saving Grace

Ingredients

1 0.75 cl (0.25 fl oz) Ben Nevis 10
1 2.1 cl (0.75 fl oz) Country Cordial (Dandelion, Aniseed,
Timut Pepper, Lemon Balm)
2.1 cl (0.75 fl oz) Fenugreek liqueur
0.75 cl (0.25 fl oz) lemon juice
2 dashes Citrus Yuzu

Method: shake • Glass: flute
Garnish: fried panko crusta rim
and 1 Rambutan in the glass

Preparation

Put all the ingredients in a shaker, fill with ice and
shake vigorously. Strain into an alabaster flute
and garnish with a hay nest.

Sazerac

Ingredients

5.7 cl (2 fl oz)
Michter's US *1
5 drops Absinthe
10 drops Peychaud's Bitters
1 sugar cube

Method: stir
Glass: double rocks
Garnish: orange twist
(then discarded)

Preparation

Fill the serving glass with ice
and a few drops of absinthe. Leave
to cool and develop flavor. Put the
sugar cube in a mixing glass
and soak it with Peychaud's bitters,
add a splash of soda and wait for it
to dissolve. Add the spirits and ice,
stir vigorously to chill the mixture.
Now empty the serving glass and
pour' in the drink. Fragrance
with a slice of orange twist;
do not garnish.

Smook Bloody

Ingredients

3 cl (1 fl oz) Kilchoman 100%
Islay
3 cl (1 fl oz) Worcester Sauce
2 dashes Tabasco Chipotle
sauce
0.35 cl (0.125 fl oz) liquid sugar
17 cl (0.125 fl oz) Datterini
tomato juice
1.5 cl (0.5 fl oz) lime juice

Method: throwing
Glass: highball
Garnish: lemon twist

Preparation

Put all the ingredients in half
a Boston shaker and fill 3/4
of the other half with ice.
Pass the liquid from one
shaker to the other, keeping
the ice in just one of them
(throwing technique). Pour
into a highball glass filled
with ice and garnish with
lime twist.

Ingredients

3 cl (1 fl oz) Nikka Coffey Malt
2.1 cl (0.75 fl oz) pink grapefruit juice
1.5 cl (0.5 fl oz) Earl Grey tea syrup
1.5 cl (0.5 fl oz) apple juice

Method: shake • Glass: sour glass

Sol Levante

Preparation

Put all the ingredients in a shaker,
fill with ice cubes and shake vigorously.
Double strain into a chilled cocktail coupe glass
and complete with a large ice cube.

Tyrannie Whisky

Ingredients

4.3 cl (1.5 fl oz) Auchentoshan Virgin Oak
1.5 cl (0.5 fl oz) Fernet
2.1 cl (0.75 fl oz) Branca Menta
3 cl (1 fl oz) lemon juice
1.5 cl (0.5 fl oz) Orgeat syrup
2 dashes Angostura Orange Bitters

Method: shake • Glass: tumbler
Garnish: lemon twist

Preparation

Put all the ingredients in a shaker, fill with ice and shake vigorously. Strain into a tumbler filled with ice, then fragrance and garnish with a slice of lemon twist.

Biographies

Davide Terziotti is a passionate expert on distilled spirits, a world to which he has dedicated studies, initiatives and research. Since 2009, he has been writing the blog "Angel's Share - Le radici, le persone e lo spirito dei distillati." In 2014, he co-founded Whiskey Club Italia, which aims to disseminate culture and knowledge on quality distilled spirits through events, courses, festivals and publishing projects.

Claudio Riva is the founder of Whiskey Club Italia, and for many years he has devoted much of his time and energy on popularizing the world of spirits. He has translated several books on whiskey into Italian, and has a keen interest in American microdistilleries.

Fabio Petroni studied photography and then collaborated with the most talented professionals in the industry. His line of work led him to specialize in portraits and still life, areas in which he has shown an intuitive and rigorous style. He works with major advertising agencies and has participated in numerous campaigns for prestigious companies known worldwide, including major Italian brands.

Erik Viola began his career in the restaurant industry, after having attended a hotel and catering school. After several years as an apprentice, he started working as a bartender; first in Liguria and later in Milan. His work experience includes the Peck Italian Bar and Pinch Spirits & Kitchen, where he is currently the bar manager.

Acknowledgements

Thanks to Pinch for its hospitality and support while creating the cocktails.

We would also like to thank the companies: Beija Flor, Compagnia dei Caraibi, Fine Spirits, Pernod Ricard Italia, Pellegrini, Puni, Rinaldi and Velier, and their representatives: Maurizio Cagnolati, Marco Callegari, Samuel Cesana, Jonas and Lukas Ebensperger, Emanuele Gozzini, Gabriele Rondani and Fabio Torretta, for their contribution to making this book possible.

For the revision of the texts, a thanks to: Daniela Daniele and Emiliano Orabona.

Fabio Petroni would like to thank Simone Paul Murat for introducing him to the world of whiskey.

Photo credits

Useful websites

BenRiach Curiositas 10
www.benriachdistillery.com

Kilkerran 12
www.kilkerransinglemalt.com

Kilchoman 100% Islay (8th edition)
kilchomandistillery.com

Highland Park 10 Old Viking Scar
www.highlandparkwhisky.com

Ben Nevis 10
www.bennevisdistillery.com

Bruichladdich Bere Barley 2009
www.bruichladdich.com

Green Spot Single Pot Still
www.spotwhiskey.com

Connemara 12
www.kilbeggandistillingcompany.com

Widow Jane Straight Bourbon
widowjane.com

Koval Four Grain
www.koval-distillery.com

Sonoma 2nd Chance Wheat
www.sonomadistillingcompany.com

Four Roses Single Barrel
fourrosesbourbon.com

Masterson's 10 Years Old Straight Rye
www.mastersonsrye.com

Chichibu Floor Malted
www.facebook.com/ChichibuDistillery/
about

Eddu Silver
www.distillerie.bzh

Slyrs Single Malt
slyrs.com

Tormore 16
www.tormoredistillery.com

anCnoc 12
ancnoc.com

Auchentoshan Virgin Oak
www.auchentoshan.com

Springbank 10
springbank.scot

Girvan Patent Still N° 4 Apps
www.thegirvanpatentstill.com

Lagavulin 12 2017
www.malts.com/en-row/distilleries/
lagavulin

Glenfarclas 15
glenfarclas.com

Nikka Coffey Malt
www.nikka.com

Yoichi Single Malt
www.nikka.com/eng/distilleries/yoichi

Glann ar mor Single Malt
glannarmor.com

Compass Box Spice Tree
www.compassboxwhisky.com

Arran Amarone Cask Finish
www.arranwhisky.com

Balblair 2005
www.balblair.com

Balvenie 12 Single Barrel
www.thebalvenie.com

Glendronach 12 Years Old
www.glendronachdistillery.com

Old Pulteney 12
www.oldpulteney.com

Teeling Small Batch Irish Whiskey
teelingwhiskey.com

Jack Daniel's Bottled in Bond Tennessee
www.jackdaniels.com

Michter's US *1 Small Batch Bourbon
michters.com

Ichiro's Malt Mizunara Wood Reserve
www.facebook.com/ChichibuDistillery/
about

Mackmyra Brukswhisky
mackmyra.com

Puni Vina
www.puni.com

Lark Cask Strength Single Malt
larkdistillery.com

Kavalan Bourbon Oak Matured
www.kavalanwhisky.com/

Project editors

VALERIA MANFERTO DE FABIANIS

LAURA ACCOMAZZO

Graphic design

MARIA CUCCHI

© 2019 White Star s.r.l.
Piazzale Luigi Cadorna, 6 - 20123 Milan, Italy
www.whitestar.it

Translation and Editing: TperTradurre s.r.l.

ISBN 978-88-544-1371-9
2 3 4 5 6   24 23 22 21 20

Printed in Croatia